LIFE 101

LIFE 101

REAL-WORLD ADVICE FOR GRADUATING COLLEGE SENIORS

PETER C. WALLACE

iUniverse, Inc.
New York Lincoln Shanghai

Life 101
Real-World Advice for Graduating College Seniors

iUniverse books may be ordered through booksellers
or by contacting:

iUniverse
2021 Pine Lake Road, Suite 100
Lincoln, NE 68512
www.iuniverse.com
1-800-Authors (1-800-288-4677)

Because of the dynamic nature of the Internet, any Web addresses or links contained in this book may have changed since publication and may no longer be valid.

The information, ideas, and suggestions in this book are not intended to render professional advice. Before following any suggestions contained in this book, you should consult your personal accountant or other financial advisor. Neither the author nor the publisher shall be liable or responsible for any loss or damage allegedly arising as a consequence of your use or application of any information or suggestions in this book.

ISBN: 978-1-58348-107-3 (pbk)
ISBN: 978-0-595-89787-2 (ebk)

Printed in the United States of America

To the three people who have journeyed with me the longest, enriched my journey in so many ways, and provided the most important ingredient in my journey—unconditional love: Annabelle, Spencer, and Terrence.

CONTENTS

PREFACE

Why do some college graduates enjoy greater success than others? How does a college graduate get started on the road to success? What are some of the keys to success in the business world? How does a young graduate begin to build his or her net worth? These and many other questions were thrown my way in 1999 when I began teaching the senior capstone course for business majors at Stonehill College.

U.S. News and World Report has ranked Stonehill College number one in its Best Northern Comprehensive Colleges—Bachelor's category for five consecutive years. Stonehill traditionally invites a practicing businessperson to teach the senior capstone business course. My predecessor, Bill Burke, did an excellent job of discussing life after graduation with his students, both individually and in the classroom. Bill encouraged me to continue to deal with the practical side of business in the classroom.

Over the course of the first two semesters, the portion of classroom activity dedicated to practical career advice evolved into what one of my students dubbed "the www sessions." The student suggested that "www" stood for "Wallace's Words of Wisdom."

During the first summer break, I began to consider the fact that so many students graduate from college without the practical tools to succeed. I had a number of in-depth conversations with my twenty-six-year-old and thirty-one-year-old sons and their friends. Based on their input, I began to review my own career.

Upon graduation from the University of Rochester in 1964 with a BS in industrial management, I started work with General Motors Corporation. I had a four-year break in the late 1960s when I served as an officer in the United States Coast Guard. Officer candidate school provided me with excellent leadership training. During my Coast Guard assignment in Puerto Rico, I was able to complete an MBA at Inter American University. Reflecting on these years provided a great deal of material for this book.

My career took off, and General Motors sponsored me for the Senior International Managers program at Harvard Business School. After completing this program, my wife and I spent about ten years living in Switzerland, Brazil, and Belgium. We moved back to the United States when I took a position with a subsidiary of Electrowatt AG, a large Swiss conglomerate. I became chairman and CEO of two of its U.S. subsidiaries. It was at this point that I became interested and active in developing young talent into skilled executives.

I retired in 1997 from ITT Corporation after a thirty-five-year career. The last ten years of my career were spent in senior operating positions. One of my strongest interests was determining how to develop and advance the careers of capable young people.

All of this experience, the content of "the www sessions," and the encouragement of my students led me to spend a summer writing this book. Its mission is simple: to provide ambitious, young college graduates with the tools to succeed. My goal is to provide an understandable framework for making the transition from college life to professional life. My hope is that some of the wisdom that I have acquired during thirty-five years of business and five years of teaching will provide clarity and direction for a new generation of successful businesspeople.

I am grateful to a number of people for their assistance in writing this book. First and foremost are the roughly six hundred students whose feedback has shaped my teaching style and the content of this book. My two sons, Mandy Scipione, and Annie Keenan read early drafts of the book and provided sage advice. Thank you all for your help.

Enjoy the book.

CHAPTER I

The Journey

> Choose a job you love, and you will never have to work a day in your life.
> Confucius (551–479 BC), Chinese philosopher

> Work is life, you know, and without it, there's nothing but fear and insecurity.
> John Lennon (1940–80), British rock musician, *Twenty-Four Hours*, originally aired on December 15, 1969, BBC TV

The Journey to Date

Many years ago, my wife introduced me to the concept of life as a journey. It is a useful concept to me because it accommodates the passage of time and the connections between the many experiences of life.

A typical college student's journey might be described as follows. One of your first scholastic memories is of the early fall morning when Mom or Dad looked at you with a funny combination of happiness and sadness, dressed you in new clothes and new shiny sneakers, put a lunch box in your hand, and ushered you off to your first day of school. If you think back, you can remember the awe and fear that struck when you realized that you were on your own with fifteen or twenty other post-toddlers in the custody of a

1

totally new adult. During some notable transitions in the past sixteen or seventeen years, you have repeated the same process. As we reflect back on the journey, we realize that we all had some tough moments. Difficult transitions included the inevitable moves from grammar school to junior high school and from junior high to high school. The timeless and popular urban legend is that the older kids in high school prey on the younger kids. This legend may have caused us enormous uncertainty and perhaps some real stress in those first few days of high school. The college transition involved no significant physical threats, but weren't we all more than a little concerned about our abilities to do college-level work? Freshman orientation and the first day of classes confirmed our fears that college was going to be hard. We also discovered that there were a large number of very smart students at our respective colleges. Most juniors and seniors can look back on the transitional phases of their academic journeys and proudly say that they succeeded in meeting those challenges.

There were also some wonderful experiences during these years: learning to read, developing your social side, making friends, participating in sports, having a teacher who stretched your intellect, and being recognized in multiple ways for your achievements.

This book hopes to help you in your next transition, which is another major step in your journey. If we can describe the first twenty years of your journey as "the learning years," then the next thirty to forty years of your journey will be "the doing years." You will now add value to the world as you continue to learn. This new phase of your journey is characterized by the expansion of two major parameters: (1) uncertainty and (2) the range and latitude of decision making that you are permitted. How you handle the uncertain future and the decisions you make will greatly influence the amount of happiness and satisfaction that you derive from your journey.

Locate a Place to Start Your Journey: Take an Inventory

Let's return to first grade again. "What do you want to be when you grow up?" the teacher asked. Heartfelt answers ranged from a basketball player, to an astronaut, to a member of a religious order, to the ever-popular president of the United States. Because you have grown up, now is an excellent time to ask that question again. This new transition is as difficult as changing from a toddler to a schoolchild, changing from a child to a teenager, or changing from a high school student to a college student. What do you want to be when you grow up?

Workforce Motivation

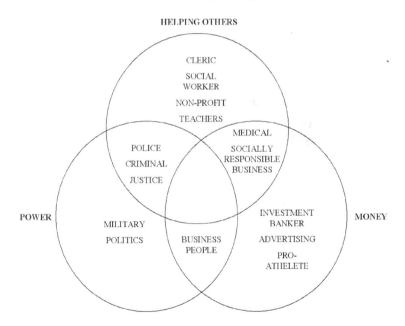

HELPING OTHERS

CLERIC
SOCIAL WORKER
NON-PROFIT
TEACHERS

MEDICAL
SOCIALLY RESPONSIBLE BUSINESS

POLICE
CRIMINAL
JUSTICE

POWER

MILITARY
POLITICS

BUSINESS PEOPLE

INVESTMENT BANKER
ADVERTISING
PRO-ATHELETE

MONEY

My students have found this diagram to be useful when reflecting on what they want to do after graduation. The information in the diagram is based on my observations, which are not supported by any scientific evidence. My hypothesis is that people are motivated to work by three main forces:

- The need to earn money
- The need to exercise power
- The need to help others

Let's walk through a few examples of how this diagram might help you.

If your main concern is the welfare of others, then you belong in the top circle. People such as clerics, social workers, teachers, and nonprofit workers belong in this circle. Some of my students argue that artists and musicians, particularly in the early phases of their careers, belong here.

Down and to the right is the intersection of people who are interested in both earning money and helping others. The medical profession most often comes up in classroom discussions. Professionals who work for businesses with a strong sense of social responsibility (such as Ben and Jerry's, Patagonia, and Whole Foods) belong in this category. Many attorneys also belong in this area.

People who are motivated primarily by money belong solely in the money circle. Investment bankers, advertising executives, and professional athletes often fall into this category.

As we continue clockwise around the diagram, we find the intersection of power and money. Businesspeople are the first professionals that I place in this section, but many successful people pursuing other organizational endeavors often find that they are motivated by both power and money.

People primarily interested in power are often involved in the military or in politics.

Finally, at the intersection of power and helping others, we find people such as police officers and other criminal justice professionals.

The center of the chart is intentionally left blank. It is the place where we all would like to be. It represents a position of power, where we are able to contribute positively to society and earn enough money to live comfortably. Getting to the center is all about choosing the place where we are most comfortable starting our respective journeys.

Think about yourself. Where are you comfortable starting your journey as an adult? Do you have a strong desire to control resources and the destinies of people? If so, begin with a profession that relates to power. Do you feel comfortable working for others' interests and bettering their lives? Pick a profession that relates to helping others. Is it important for you to live comfortably and to provide for yourself and your family in a comfortable manner? Select a profession in the money segment.

Then, as you move through your journey, try to add pieces from' the other segments in the diagram to your life and move ever closer to the center of the rings. Though oversimplified, this may be a helpful way to select a starting point for your journey.

The Future Journey

The wonderful and perhaps slightly scary thing about your next step into the working world is that you are now in control of the journey. You will never be totally alone, but most of what you will accomplish in the next forty or fifty years will be shaped by the goals you set, by the risks you take, and by the companions you select for your journey. The most important point of this chapter is that the journey is yours to manage. To this point in your journey, you have been shaped by the decisions of other people: caring parents, teachers, coaches, and religious advisors.

You are now the captain of your own ship. Be decisive and go for what *you* want. Take careful counsel, but make your own decisions. Simply put, you are now an adult. You now have custody of your own destiny.

CHAPTER II

Success and Uncertainty

Self-trust is the first secret of success.
Ralph Waldo Emerson, *Success*

We sail within a vast sphere, ever drifting in uncertainty,
driven from end to end.
Blaise Pascal, *Pensées, no. 72*

Decisions, decisions, and decisions. Are you uncertain about your career choice? Uncertain about whether you should read this chapter? Success will depend on your ability to deal with uncertainty.

In this chapter we will discuss uncertainty and think about how to deal with it. To me, uncertainty has been the greatest challenge of adulthood. All decisions are made with some degree of uncertainty. The risk/reward ratio is entirely based on uncertainty. Uncertainty plays a major role in negotiations. Personally, I am comfortable with the uncertainty in our environment, which seems, to me, to be uncontrollable. I don't spend much time worrying about whether the earth will be hit by a meteor in the next two hundred years, whether I will win the lottery, or whether the world is going to end this week. Those big issues are fun to ponder, but they don't upset me. I also don't worry too much about the little stuff. If I lose a few bucks playing golf or if someone is late for one of my classes, the stakes are so small that it does not bother me.

The Uncertainty and Decision Matrix

Uncertainty can be better understood if we try to understand the size of the stakes in question and the person or people who control the decision processes. I choose the word *stakes* because there are both material and emotional consequences to most decisions.

I developed the following matrix to illustrate my ideas. The vertical axis indicates who has control of the process. The top of the vertical axis is where we are in control of the decision making, and the bottom of the vertical axis is where some anonymous person controls the decisions. We are more comfortable allowing others to make decisions for us when they are people we trust, such as parents, loved ones, or good friends. The more remote the decision makers are, the more our discomfort increases.

On the horizontal axis we have the size of the stakes, either material or emotional, going from trivial stakes on the left to high stakes on the right.

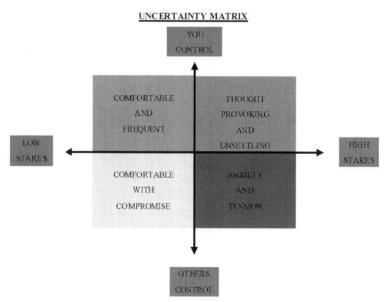

UNCERTAINTY MATRIX

YOU CONTROL

	COMFORTABLE AND FREQUENT	THOUGHT PROVOKING AND UNSETTLING	
LOW STAKES			HIGH STAKES
	COMFORTABLE WITH COMPROMISE	ANXIETY AND TENSION	

OTHERS CONTROL

Let me introduce the above chart with a familiar example. Sometime in the middle of our high school experiences, we started to explore the idea of going to college. Most of us started the process with a number of conversations. We consulted counselors, spoke with our teachers, talked with our family members, and perhaps even met with some college students we knew. We formed some vague impressions about what we wanted to be or do. We made the decision to explore going to college.

At this point, we entered the upper left-hand area of the above chart, labeled "Comfortable and Frequent." We were going to examine various colleges and make some general selections. Because of the large number of colleges in the United States and the wide variety of choices, we were in control of the process, and the stakes were relatively low.

We then discovered that we had to take a competitive nationwide test in order to apply to college. The test would compare our abilities against those of our peers nationwide. The stakes became a good deal higher; however, we were in control of the process. We entered the zone in the upper right-hand corner. Most of us studied hard and took the sample tests, which gave us some control over the process. It was unsettling and yet exciting to know that we would compete on a national level.

At some point during the process, generally after we had received our test scores, we narrowed our college choices. At this point, we began to get a great deal of advice. Many of us decided to visit several colleges, and, in most cases, one or both of our parents tagged along. Most of us wanted to be in the "Thought Provoking and Unsettling" zone of uncertainty—in other words, we wanted to be in control of this high-stakes decision. But, for many of us, we also crossed into the "Comfortable with Compromise" quadrant. During the college visits, parents wanted to ask questions, visit academic buildings, see dorm rooms, and understand the policies of the school. To most of us, these were low-stakes items, so we often sat back and indulged our parents because it was clear that they also wanted some control over the process. During these visits, we were often in both the unsettling and comfortable zones.

Then, crunch time came, and we selected a small number of colleges to apply to. We were edging out of the lower left-hand quadrant and toward the final quadrant. We worked on essays, filled out applications, retook the national tests, and did everything we could to control our fate. Sometime in December or January, the process was complete, and we mailed our applications.

On the day that we sent out the applications, we entered deep into the "Anxiety and Tension" zone. We had nagging questions. Will I get into any school? What if I don't get into the one I want? Which one do I want anyway? Who gave those anonymous admissions officers the right to judge me? As the March 1 deadline approached, the anxiety ratcheted up, and the tension was high. There were noontime phone calls to home. Did the mail come? Any mail from any colleges? Is the envelope fat or thin?

Then the first acceptance letter arrived. The pain of the rejection letters faded quickly, but most of us will remember the first acceptance letter forever. We thought that the process was over because the uncertainty had been removed. We were going to college. Then, for most of us, a second acceptance came in, and perhaps even more.

We moved right back onto the uncertainty chart and into the unsettling quadrant. We were back in control, but we had to make a big, high-stakes decision: which college do I attend? After much thought and much discussion, we finally made the biggest decision of our lives at that time. We had successfully navigated through all four quadrants of the uncertainty matrix and arrived at a decision.

Let's examine the characteristics of decisions in each quadrant. Let's start with the quadrant in the upper left-hand corner. This quadrant represents the type of uncertainty that we face when making daily, routine decisions. It rarely causes us much stress or anxiety. This is where we live every day. We make hundreds of decisions daily. When we walk into the college cafeteria, the local pizzeria, or a fast-food franchise, we need to make a decision. There is very little uncertainty because we have eaten this type of food hundreds of times before; we understand what we want, and we act. Clearly, this is a stress-free decision—unless we think about it. What if we are on a diet? What if we are worried about the ingredients in the food, or what if we are allergic to something? Our control of the situation declines, and the stakes go up. Uncertainty rears its head, and anxiety increases.

How about the upper right-hand quadrant? It illustrates the more stressful nature of the decisions made in this quadrant. A good example here might be the decision to buy a car. The stakes are high because we are going to spend a lot of money and because we intend to use the car for an extended length of time. When deciding whether to purchase the car, we need to consider multiple criteria—acquisition cost, reliability, operating cost, and image, to name a few. We are also uncertain about our ability to negotiate. To enhance our feeling of control, we can do research. To minimize the stakes, we can negotiate from a position of strength. We make relatively few of these decisions in our lifetime; however, many of them are defining moments in our journey.

The lower left-hand quadrant illustrates situations where the stakes are not very high but where other people are in control. These decisions are stressful not because of the stakes but because of our reluctance to cede control to others. Many of these decisions affect our relationships with others. An example might be the classic dilemma that a couple faces when selecting a movie. He wants an action flick with lots of chase scenes and a good measure of physical conflict. She wants a romantic comedy with some emotional content that will provoke a good laugh and perhaps a tear. Both people feel that it is important to attend the same movie and to be with each other. Someone has to cede control of the situation. Couples frequently resolve this situation by alternating the types of movies or events that they attend. Too much concession by one party increases the stress on the relationship. Each day, there are countless situations like this in the workplace. Operating in this environment requires tact and an ability to subjugate our natural desire for control in order to achieve the more important goals of harmony and cooperation.

Finally, let us examine the lower right-hand zone. The circumstances in this quadrant are the most difficult. Here, we are not the decision makers, and the outcomes of the decisions are very important to us. Consider the situation that occurs when we participate in a competitive tryout. It could be a tryout for an athletic team, a debate team, a musical ensemble, a theatrical event, or a scholarship. Outsiders, whom we barely know, are the judges. The uncertainty surrounding these events is stressful. During the period of uncertainty, we ruminate about the outcome of the tryout. We often sway between being confident that we will be selected and trying to convince ourselves that we are indifferent to the outcome. This type of uncertainty is the most difficult to handle. We can influence the outcome by doing our best, but, once the trials are over, we can only sit and wait. We can reduce the importance of the stakes by seeking alternatives if we are rejected, but that is often difficult to do. This type of uncertainty becomes a major factor in living life as an adult. In business, uncertainty will surround promotions, raises, bonuses, or generating new business for your firm. In life, it will surround decisions about changing jobs and starting your own business.

Risk/Reward

One of the fundamental concepts of business in a capitalist economy is that rewards are proportional to the risk taken. Risk is essentially uncertainty. The less we know about the outcome of a venture, the higher the risk.

A simple example of this can be found in the game of roulette. At a roulette table, there are thirty-eight numbers: the numbers one through thirty-six, a single zero, and a double zero. The thirty-six numbers are colored black and red; the odd numbers are red, and the even numbers are black. A low-risk bet is a bet on black or red; you have a 47 percent chance of winning, and, if you win, you double your money. There are other escalating payoffs until you get to the most risky bet—a bet on a single number. You have a 2.6 percent chance of winning that bet (on average, you will win about once every forty times that you bet on a single number), but, if you win, you multiply your money thirty-six times. In each case, if you do not select correctly, you lose your bet. So the higher the risk you are willing to take, the higher the reward.

In life, we deal with risk and reward all the time; sometimes we understand the risk, but sometimes we do not. Many decisions that you make in your life will be based on the uncertainty (or perceived risk) of a situation and what it may yield you. There are some fundamental techniques for handling decisions that I would like to pass on to you.

First, the uncertainty matrix suggests that if the stakes are larger, then both the risk and the potential reward are higher. This should lead each of us to the conclusion that, for decisions with high stakes, we should make an all-out effort to get information regarding the outcome. In-depth research on big decisions can lead to significant insight as to whether the risk is worth the potential reward.

Second, the more remote the people involved in the decisions, the greater the uncertainty of the outcome. This should lead each of us to the conclusion that, in situations where the stakes are high, we should try to get to know the decision makers. In the case of our college admission director, we could not take such an action. Too often, especially in business, people are unwilling to engage in dialogue with decision makers about such important things as their career directions, compensation, or other key issues. This leaves the decision maker uninformed and leaves the person in a constant state of uncertainty because he or she has been too timid to approach the decision maker.

Third, one must accept that the journey is going to be uncertain. How boring would life be if we knew every twist and turn in our journey? Part of the excitement of being adults is that our lives are filled with uncertainty. We are empowered to manage the risks associated with the uncertainty and to reap the rewards of risk taking. Two things have been important to me while dealing with uncertainty:

- Do not overthink decisions. Become informed and then decide. Trust your gut instinct. Most business executives will admit that if they make the right decision more than half the time, they are satisfied.

- Do not second-guess yourself. As Yogi Berra said, "When you come to a fork in the road, take it." You can never know the outcome of selecting other alternatives in a decision; if things turn out poorly, move on. Many people dwell on past decisions and miss out on potential future opportunities.

Finally, when you are in a position to supervise other people, they will perform better if you minimize the uncertainty in their environment. You will be a well-respected and successful leader if you clearly communicate your expectations, outline the rules for evaluating job performance, and transmit information in a timely manner.

CHAPTER III

Moving On

There is not any present moment that is unconnected with some future one. The life of every man is a continued chain of incidents, each link of which hangs upon the former. The transition from cause to effect, from event to event, is often carried on by secret steps, which our foresight cannot divine, and our sagacity is unable to trace.

Joseph Addison (1672–1719), British essayist, "Happiness Not Independent" and *Poetical Fragments, Interesting Anecdotes, Memoirs, Allegories, Essays* (1794)

The transition from college to the outside world provides each new adult with a greater degree of decision making and control. We might pause and conclude that if we have more control, then things are going to be easier and more certain. The truth, of course, is quite the opposite. We are faced with so many new decisions and so much new information that we can often feel overwhelmed. The balance of this book is filled with guidelines that my students have found useful when making the transition from college to the "real world."

At some point during your senior year, it is going to occur to you that you have to get a job. For many of my students, this knowledge gnaws at them for months before they take any action. For others, it is an issue that they choose to ignore, or they calculate that they will ease into something after graduation. The majority of my students, however, recognize that this is the first step in managing their lives, and they work at finding a job.

Regrettably, I have known only a few students who have put as much effort into finding a job as they put into getting into college. After reflecting on this, I believe it is a direct result of parents not nagging them to get things done. Finding a job is the start of the rest of your life and the key to complete independence; it should be the number one priority during your senior year. One of my students said, "Taking responsibility for the job search is crucial to growing up."

Job Hunting

The first place to start is at the career center at your college or university. I am aware that career centers at many campuses have earned, unfairly, poor reputations. The reason for this is that graduates who do not get a job while in college hold the career centers responsible for their failures.

You must have the proper attitude when visiting a career center. Keep the following four points in mind:

- The career center exists to support you in your job search, not to hand you a job.
- The career center is composed of multitasking people who want to work with well-organized job seekers. Your tuition pays their salaries, so you should get as much help from them as possible.
- *You* are responsible for getting assistance from them and finding your own job.
- Familiarize yourself with the career center during the second semester of your junior year.

Step 1: Define what you want to do. Chapter I may be useful in this endeavor. If you always wanted to be a ski instructor, go do it. A student of mine worked as a ski instructor in Vermont and Chile for two years. He had a great time, and, after returning to his alma mater, several of his professors and career-center advisors helped him get a job as a salesperson in the recreational sports field. He is happy and has satisfied the itch to be a ski instructor. If you always dreamed of being a professional bungee jumper, then now is the time in your life to do it.

If, on the other hand, you are like the majority of people and are ready to begin a professional career, then define what it is that you want to do. Perhaps you have a preprofessional degree and have found a vocation you enjoy. Clearly, then, you are going to search for a job as a teacher, a social worker, a law enforcement officer, an accountant, an engineer, or a health-care professional. This is an enormous help because it gives you focus. If you do not have a clue about what you want to do, sit down with someone in the career services center, and he or she will help you focus. Many people know only what they do *not* want to do. Parents, relatives, and professors are also valuable sources of insight on what professional areas might be appealing to you.

Make a decision. Decide on an area of focus for your job search. In the modern world, with the accelerated rate of change in the employment market, it is highly unlikely that your lifetime vocation will be defined by your first job. In today's world, employees and employers are constantly reinventing themselves, so you need not feel constrained by your choice. But choose you must, because no employer is going to hire you if you do not appear to know yourself well enough to articulate what it is that you want to do.

© 1997 Randy Glasbergen
www.glasbergen.com

"I believe in paying my employees as much
as they need. Since you'll be working
90 hours a week, you won't need much."

Step 2: Capture your talent and know-how on a single piece of paper. This is the résumé. Career services can be a great deal of help here. Here are some hints:

- *Develop your own brand image.* Your name and addresses lines should be the same on all correspondence (résumé, letterhead, e-mail, reference list). The header should be appropriate for your profession and consistent throughout.

- *Do not use template-type résumés, such as those in software packages.* Recruiters see too many of these, and they make you look like one of the herd.

- *Be immodest.* Find unique, positive things about your life, and bring them out in your résumé or in your cover letter. Interviewers want something interesting to talk about. Salt your résumé with a few themes that can create such a conversation.

- *Highlight things that are appropriate to the job focus you have chosen.* Emphasize any accomplishments, prizes and honors, or work-related experience you have had. I once got a good marketing job with an automotive company because my future boss was impressed that I had worked as a car salesman for a few weeks before the interview.

- *Show your résumé to a few people.* Advisors from the career services center, professors in the field of focus, and relatives are all candidates. They will have conflicting advice. You are in charge—take the advice that you like and finalize *your* résumé.

- *Do not let the process go on forever.* A favorite way for job hunters to procrastinate is by spending a lot of time refining their résumés; a couple of weeks is enough time—more than a month is too long.

Step 3: Network with people in your desired job field. This advice is the hardest to take. A student of mine told me that she could never, ever, do it. I hounded her for months to do it because she had a great contact. Finally, to get me off her back, she networked with her contact and found her ideal job.

Networking is the art of enrolling other people in your job search. It is really hard because no one, me included, likes to ask others for help. In my thirty-four-year business career, I must have provided contacts for hundreds of people who networked with me. I enjoyed doing it and never felt put-upon. However, when it came time for me to change jobs, I had the hardest time starting the networking process. Two of the best jobs of my career came directly from networking. Experts agree that about 75 percent of managerial and professional jobs are never advertised or posted by employers. The conclusion must be that networking is the most effective way to find a job.

Networking is a simple process:

- *Identify a small number of people, ten or fewer, whom you know and who have some relationship to your chosen field.* The more senior these people are in their organizations, the better, but you must make a list. Obvious sources are relatives (What about that aunt who just got a promotion at an accounting firm?), neighbors (What about the engineer, architect, or doctor who lives across the street?), youth coaches and teachers (What about your high school English teacher who does social service during the summer?), and former employers (What about the body shop owner who deals every day with insurance companies?). Most college career services centers maintain lists of alumni who are willing to help job seekers; these individuals are excellent networking sources.

- *Prepare for the contact.* Learn as much as you can about their companies. Have clear goals in mind.

- *Next comes the hard, hard part: make contact.* Try for a person-to-person contact, even if you have to settle for a telephone conversation. Be clear, but indirect, in your opening statement. You can say something like, "Hello. This is Peter Wallace calling; you were my lacrosse coach in junior high. I will be graduating from PU this spring and am interested in a career in marketing. I remember that you are a successful marketing manager and wonder if I could meet with you at your office sometime to discuss my career?" **Note: you never ask if they have a job for you.** If they have job openings, they will let you know soon enough; if they do not and you ask, then it will be the end of the conversation. Assume that, of the ten people you call, about half will be willing to help. The help will come in several ways:

1. Your contact may invite you to visit the workplace or ask you to meet for lunch. The latter is the best situation. Prepare for the lunch by generating a series of questions about the profession you have selected. Also prepare to ask your host how he or she got started in this career. Your goal for this lunch is to tap into your host's network and get the names and telephone numbers of people who may help you in your job hunt. Ask your host if you may use his or her name when contacting the suggested people.

2. Your contact may request that you provide a résumé that could be circulated among colleagues. Agree, of course, but ask the contact if you may call back in one week to obtain a list of the people who received your résumé; be sure to get their contact information (e.g., e-mail address, phone number). This does three things: it keeps the door open with the contact, it sets a deadline, and it permits you to have new networking contacts for follow-up purposes.

3. Your contact may also request your résumé and forward it to the company's human resources department. Again, try to set a deadline and get a name to contact directly.

- *Follow up the contact.* Follow up with your host, and thank him or her for the time and hospitality. Remember, the header on your letter or e-mail should reflect your brand.

Finally, get in touch with people on your newly acquired list of names. Now you are talking to perfect strangers. Ironically, it is easier to ask for help from strangers than from people you know. The dialogue is similar to that used with your first contact. You might say, "Hello. My name is Peter Wallace, and so and so of ABC Industries suggested that I call you. I will be graduating from PU in the spring and am interested in a career in marketing. So and so told me that you are a successful marketer and could perhaps spare some time to give me some career advice. When would it be convenient for us to talk?" Again, do not request a job; just issue a simple plea for help. If you get a cold response, you might close the conversation by asking if there is a colleague who would be willing to spend some time with you.

Networking should produce an ever-expanding web of contacts that will lead to interviews and job offers.

Keep in touch with your original contacts, and let them know how things are going. Remember: your contacts have recommended you to their business friends; they are interested in the outcome of your conversations. It is important to maintain regular contact with every member of your network.

Step 4: Consider trying the low-yield paths to getting a job.

- *On-campus interview.* Imagine for a minute that you are the interviewer—perhaps an alumnus of the college or a trained human resources professional. Your institution has decided that it will hire a small number of new college graduates. You are assigned to an interview team that will read résumés from and talk to about one hundred times more candidates than your company can hire. In other words, you are going to be looking for the really outstanding candidates.

  How can you become an outstanding candidate? In step 5, I will discuss how to handle the screening interview. In order to get the interview, you must possess the resourcefulness to sign up early for the campus interviews, and you must have a résumé that makes a fairly bored interviewer take notice. It has been my experience that signing up for the first interview of the day (when the interviewer is fresh) or the last interview of the day (when you can leave the final lasting impression) will yield the best results.

A final word on campus interviews: most companies interview recent college graduates for entry-level jobs that they have trouble filling with experienced people. In other words, they are not very desirable jobs. On-campus recruiting and hiring offers companies a chance to test a large number of people in relatively unattractive jobs and watch the cream rise. It is my view that if you rely solely on campus interviews to get your job, you'll be job hunting again in a year or two. Why not start networking now and find a job that will give you some satisfaction from the outset?

- *Internet résumé posting.* My students have had some success finding interesting jobs by posting their résumé on job sites such as Careerbuilder.com, Monster.com, and others. A simple Web search will yield more résumé sites than you can ever use. Many professional organizations also have résumé-posting sites.

- *Institutional Web sites.* Most companies and government organizations post job openings on their Web sites. This is an effective way to distribute your résumé to organizations you have targeted.

- *Direct mail.* This can be an effective way of reaching a defined target if you want a specific job and if you know that you want to work in a certain geographic area. For example, if you are seeking a job as a police officer, send your résumé and a strong, personalized cover letter to every municipality in the area. Direct mail companies are ecstatic if they get a 1 percent yield. If you send your letter to one hundred municipalities, you should feel good if you get one interview. One of my students took a temporary job in a large company as an executive assistant to the sales manager. Each week, she received about a hundred unsolicited résumés. Her job was to put them in a folder and hold them for a month in case the sales manager wanted to look at them. During the ten months that she was there, she discarded about four thousand résumés, which the sales manager never examined. She did tell me that the sales manager interviewed and hired a number of people who contacted him by networking through people that he knew. One person who was hired was the father of the sales manager's daughter's college roommate.

"Having spent the last six years of my life reading, writing and studying, I'd like to find an executive position that doesn't require any mental activity."

Step 5: Prepare for the interview. Someone, somewhere, finally agrees to talk to you and a few other people about a position. There are two types of interviews: the screening interview and the hiring interview.

- *The screening interview.* A human resources professional normally conducts this interview. Most screening interviewers have had professional interview training and see themselves as "gatekeepers." In other words, it is their job to pare down the list of job candidates that will be recommended to the hiring manager. Typically, fewer than ten people will be invited to a screening interview, and fewer than five people will be invited to the hiring interview. The screening interview normally will be thirty to sixty minutes long and will be conducted in the institution's human resources department or in an interview room on your college campus. The keys to a successful screening interview are as follows:

o **Be timely.** Arrive at least ten to fifteen minutes early. Be sure to give yourself plenty of time to find the building. If you are too early, find a coffee shop, have a cup of coffee, and read the paper. If some unforeseen circumstance delays you, notify the interviewer as far in advance as possible that you will be late. Offer to reschedule at his or her convenience.

o **Be prepared.** You should have read everything that you can get your hands on regarding the institution you are interviewing with. Web pages and Web searches are so informative these days that it is relatively easy to learn a great deal about any institution. You should prepare several key questions about the institution that will get the interviewer talking. Questions should center on positive events that have occurred in the recent past. For example, an aspiring teacher might say, "I see that your school won a grant for early intervention in reading. How do you plan to implement the program?" An applicant for a job with a corporation might ask, "I noticed that your company just changed advertising agencies. Does that mean you have some new products in the pipeline?" Another business-minded interviewee may question, "The launch of your new heat sensors seems to open up new opportunities for your company. Do you see other applications for it, aside from dishwashers?" While listening to the answers, try to formulate a way that you can relate your unique skill set to the answer. For example, a teaching applicant might respond, "During my student teaching, the principal complimented me on my ability to deal with slow readers; I believe that, in addition to my regular duties as a third-grade teacher, I could contribute to the early-intervention program." Or you might say, "It is interesting that you intend to open new markets using this new agency; my marketing background and flexibility might be useful in helping the team build the new image." An aspiring businessperson could respond, "My engineering background, combined with the business courses I took, might give me an edge in seeking new markets for heat sensors." In other words, ask topical questions and try to predict the direction the answer will take. Then, make yourself a part of the solution.

o **Have presence and poise.** Dress and act like a grown-up. Purchase some conservative business clothing, including new shoes. Footwear should consist of conservative tie shoes for men or low-heeled shoes for women, and be sure that the shoes are polished. Wear the clothes and shoes a few times before your first interview so that you feel comfortable. Be cleanly groomed. For men, that means a fresh haircut and no beard or mustache. (If you must have a mustache, it should be neatly trimmed.) For women, hair should be neatly groomed and away from the face. Do not overlook your fingernails. Men and women should neatly trim and clean under their nails. Women wearing fingernail polish should also be sure that it is applied evenly and not chipped. Be sharp and feel sharp. Don't forget to remove your baseball hats. If you smoke, abstain prior to the interview. Be sure that your breath is fresh.

o **Project your image.** Always greet your interviewer with a firm handshake and look him or her in the eye. Try and maintain as much eye contact as is comfortable during the interview. Stay focused on the interview, and, when the interviewer is talking, listen attentively. Do not interrupt. Most interviewers would rather hear themselves talk. Sit up straight, and keep both feet on the floor. Talk in a clear, loud, confident voice. Answer questions directly with short, well-thought-out answers. A professional interviewer will often ask open-ended questions such as the following:

- Can you give me an example of your leadership ability?
- What is the biggest challenge you have ever faced?
- What is your greatest strength (weakness)?

Prepare several "war stories" in advance. Think about situations in which you have been tested and have risen to the challenge, situations in which you showed leadership, and situations in which you were a good team member. Hone these stories, and then shape them to suit the questions asked.

o **Request information.** You should learn from your interviewer the specific job for which you are being considered. Try to ascertain your responsibilities, the training you will receive, and a potential career path. The interviewer may describe the institution's benefit programs and salary range. Never ask about salary at this stage, as it decreases your negotiating leverage. If you are asked what you expect to earn, give a general answer such as: "I am sure that you will provide a competitive offer commensurate with my education and experience."

o **Follow up.** Always, always, follow up an interview with an e-mail and a letter. Statistics show that only about 20 percent of job candidates send thank-you letters after an interview. Be one of the 20 percent; it really makes a difference with the potential employer. As soon as you leave the interview, write yourself a note about key parts of the interview. In your follow-up letter, thank the interviewer for his or her time and attention. If you think that you replied weakly to any interview questions, you can use the thank-you letter to improve your previous answers. If you found an area of mutual interest or if the interviewer responded positively to one part of the conversation, expand on those points.

- *The hiring interview.* If you made it through the screening interview, then you are now going to talk to your future boss. You are on a short list of probably no more than five candidates. The person you are talking to is *not* a professional interviewer. This person is an executive with all the pressures and time constraints of day-to-day operations. The steps of this interview are similar to those of the screening interview, but the decision making is much more emotional. Your interviewer is looking for someone who will fit into his or her team. We'll go over the steps again.

  o **Be timely.** Promptness is even more important for this interview. Your future boss is judging you.

  o **Be prepared.** By this time, you should have acquired a great deal of information about your future employer. If the company produces a consumer product or service, then you should have tried it and should have an opinion about it. You should be current on everything that is happening with the institution. Do a keyword search of the local newspapers to gain information on the last few months of the company's operations. Understand and be prepared to discuss the job for which you are interviewing. You should have obtained this information from your screening interview. Use your network to understand the scope of the job. Finally, see if you can identify anyone who knows your potential boss. If so, ask whether you can use this person's name as a reference. Nothing gives prospective bosses more comfort than being able to get some information on a candidate from someone they know.

  o **Have presence and poise.** Reread the paragraph above.

  o **Project an image.** This is the toughest part of this interview. The new boss is looking for someone who fits his or her image of a good employee. The boss could probably not describe that image, and you will either meet it or not. The important thing is to project the best image possible and hope that it resonates with the interviewer. Start with a firm handshake, and look the interviewer in the eye. The conversation is likely to be a bit more awkward in this interview; unlike the screener, this interviewer meets with job candidates only a few times a year. Be prepared to carry the conversation. When the interviewer asks if you have any questions, use your preparation to ask intelligent questions about the current environment. Be interested in the mission of the institution and its current situation. If you can get the interviewer talking about his or her work and about the company's mission, you are likely to have a successful interview. While trying to get a glimpse of you as a person, the interviewer may relax a bit with you and ask about sports and hobbies—follow this lead. When discussing these areas, strive to emphasize your leadership ability and that you are a team player. Only refer to yourself if questioned directly.

o **Ask one final question.** Near the end of the interview, you should ask, "Is there anything more I could tell you that would help you as you decide whom to hire for this job?" You may get a hint of the viability of your candidacy.

o **Follow up.** Again, make notes, particularly about areas in which the interviewer was interested. See if you can do some quick research about a topic. Write an e-mail and a hard copy thank-you letter to the interviewer, amend any parts of the interview that you think needed attention, and enclose any topical research that you may have found. Finally, close the letter by indicating your interest in taking the job. Send a blind copy of the letter to the screening interviewer.

Step 6: Consider the job offers. Searching for a job is like applying to college: when the first offer comes in, the uncertainty evaporates, and you are back in control. There are several things to consider at this point:

- The screening interviewer may call and inform you that you are going to get a written offer, or you may be invited back to the organization to receive the offer. In either case, the institution will probably establish a deadline for your acceptance. At this point, you have the fish on the hook, and you want to reel it in slowly. Be enthusiastic about the offer, and let them know that you will require a bit of time to discuss the offer with your advisors.

- If you have been working diligently at finding a job, you should have several other prospects in the works when you get your first offer. If the first offer is your dream job and the other prospects pale by comparison, take the first offer—don't waste your time or the time of the other institutions. Terminate the other prospects with a phone call and a follow-up e-mail, and thank them for their efforts. Be sure to notify your network that you are out of play. Thank every member of your network, and maintain a list of their contact numbers. They represent potential networking candidates for your next job search.

- On the other hand, if you have prospects that look more attractive, it is time to get a bit more aggressive. Call your contacts at each of the attractive prospects. Inform them that you have a firm job offer, and let them know that you have a deadline. They will either thank you politely or speed up their process in order to meet your deadline. It is a good way to separate the people who are serious about you from those who are not. It is often possible to return to the institution that gave you the first offer and get an extension. Be sure that the extension is sufficient, because you should ask for only one.

- When sorting through multiple offers, you should try to establish some rational basis for comparison. My students find the reputation of the institution, geography, job content, personality of the boss, and perceived opportunity to be realistic criteria. Notice that I did not mention salary; I'll get to that.

I want to include a brief story here. One of my students did all of the above analysis and eliminated all but two offers. Because the offers were so similar, she decided to select between the finalists by flipping a coin. She flipped the coin, and, when faced with the result, she decided that she wanted to flip again and go with the best two out of three. Of course, she didn't flip again; she happily went to work for the company that lost the first coin flip. Sometimes you know in your gut where you want to work, but it takes a coin flip to get to the truth.

Suppose that you have decided where you want to go to work but that you are troubled because they are not paying the highest salary. The first step is to call the institution. Inform the institution that you are very interested in the job but that you have another job offer for more money. State the amount of the higher offer; be accurate, and do not be dishonest. Provide them with some incentive by stating that you are prepared to work for them if they can match the salary. Generally the company will consider your request. They will either increase their offer or remain firm. If they are unable to meet the higher salary but you still love the job, then go to work there; you will have established your worth and be in a position to ask for more money at a future date.

In almost all cases, employers expect you to negotiate for a higher salary. Make a reasonable request in a businesslike way. Even if the employer declines to give you an increase at this time, you establish your expectations for an early review of your salary.

There are three important steps in the wrap-up. First, inform all other institutions that you have accepted another offer, and thank them for their interest. Second, inform and thank all the members of your network. Third, make a summary of all the people you contacted, and include their current contact information. This is the foundation of the network for your next job search. Store this information in a safe place.

CHAPTER IV

Budgeting

> Money is just a bunch of green fun coupons; let's enjoy.
> Bill Wallace, my brother

> Money is of no value; it cannot spend itself.
> All depends on the skill of the spender.
> Ralph Waldo Emerson (1803–82), speech, February 7, 1844, the
> Mercantile Library Association, Boston, Massachusetts, "The
> Young American," *Nature, Addresses, and Lectures* (1849)

Well, now you have a job, and you're ready to move out of college and be on your own. The dream, of course, is to get a nice two-bedroom apartment with a view. Two bedrooms will accommodate all of your friends from college, who can visit you for those awesome parties you are going to throw. Also, you must have a sharp set of wheels—something along the lines of a Beemer 300, Jeep Wrangler, or a Corvette. You need to improve your wardrobe and get some good-looking threads for work and play. Finally, you'll have enough money to attend some really good concerts, to travel around the world to see all your friends, and to pay off the credit cards—and you might consider putting your extra money away for a rainy day. Sound good? Let's take a look. The first thing to do in any short-term financial situation is to come up with a budget. A budget worksheet might look something like this:

MONTHLY BUDGET

Income:
Monthly Salary   _____
Withholding (28% of monthly salary)   _____
Net Income   _____

Expenses:

     <u>Housing</u>
     Rent   _____
     Electricity   _____
     Heat   _____
     Water   _____
     Gas   _____
     Cable Television   _____
     Telephone   _____
     Cellular Telephone   _____
         Subtotal Housing   _____
     <u>Automotive</u>
     Loan Payments   _____
     Insurance   _____
     Gasoline   _____
     Maintenance   _____
         Subtotal Automotive   _____

     <u>Commuting</u>   _____

     <u>Personal Costs</u>
     Breakfast   _____
     Lunch   _____
     Dinner   _____
     Laundry and Dry Cleaning   _____
     Personal Hygiene, Cosmetics, and Grooming   _____
     Credit Card Payments   _____
     Student Loan Repayments   _____
         Subtotal Personal Costs   _____
             Total Fixed Monthly Costs   _____

Net Income minus Total Monthly Fixed Costs or Money for Fun and Saving

---

We will work through an example just so we can get a flavor of what things are going to look like.

Let's assume that you have a starting salary at about the national mean of $36,000 a year. We can quickly calculate our available net income.

Income:

Monthly Salary	$3,000
Withholding (28% of monthly salary)	$ 840
Net Income	**$2,160**

You will get a more accurate number when you get your first paycheck. The amount that your employer requires you to contribute to your health insurance premium will be a factor and could decrease this amount. A point to remember here is that you are likely to be paid twice a month. This means you must hold enough cash from the payment in the middle of the month to cover all the bills that will be due at the end of the month. It is a common mistake to feel very well-off during the last part of the month and very poor during the beginning of the month when all the bills are due.

The first big decision that you must make concerns housing. The dream of renting a two-bedroom apartment on your own will quickly fade when you check rental costs; this is especially true if your job takes you to a large urban area. In major metropolitan areas, two-bedroom apartments range from $2,500 to $3,500 a month—clearly not in your range. You'll probably need one or several roommates; your college buddies are good candidates. For a shared apartment or house, it is reasonable for each person to pay between $600 and $1,000 per month. We'll use the midpoint, $800, as a working number. Electricity is about $70 per month, but it can cost more in warmer climates where you will use more air-conditioning. Heat, on the other hand, will not be a factor in the South, but in the North it can run several hundred dollars a month during the winter. For our example, let's assume that the heating bill is only $60 per month. If your landlord does not pay for water, it should cost no more than $20 per month. If your dwelling is connected to natural gas, you can expect to pay an additional $20 per month for cooking and hot water. Cable television can run between $30 and $50, depending on the level of service. Finally, one of the greatest variables in the budget is the telephone. A hardwired telephone with local service will cost about $30 per month, but the cost can skyrocket if you make a lot of long-distance calls. Most of you have cellular telephones; I will include $50 in the budget for your personal cell phone. Let's assume that you will have one roommate. After halving all the costs, except cell phone costs, the housing expenses look as follows:

Housing

Rent	800
Electricity	35
Heat	30
Water	10
Gas	10
Cable Television	15
Telephone	15
Cellular Telephone	50
Subtotal Housing	**965**

It appears that somewhere between 40 percent and 50 percent of your monthly salary is going to go toward a place to live. You still have $1,195 left.

Let's move on to automotive costs. Later in the book, in Appendix B, we will discuss buying a car. For the moment, let us assume that you have decided that, after all the hard work of college, you deserve a new car. Although you would love to buy that new

Beemer, you have decided to restrict yourself to $20,000. You're willing to borrow the money for five years, at which time you will own a five-year-old car. Assuming an interest rate of 5.0 percent, your monthly payment will be $377.42 per month. In Chapter V, which discusses financial leverage, I will show you how to use the Internet to calculate these numbers. Insurance is a variable that depends on your age, the type of car, and your driving record, but I will assume that you will pay $1,800 per year, or $150 per month. You can obtain a quote from numerous Internet sites or by calling any insurance company. If you plan to use your car to get back and forth to work, you'll probably use a tank of gas each week. Gasoline currently runs about $25 per tank, so you'll need at least $100 each month. You have to change the oil, but little else is required for the first year or so; I will allocate $10 a month for maintenance. But, if you buy a used car with more than fifty thousand miles, you had better allocate about $100 per month for maintenance. New tires, brake linings, tune-ups, and new exhaust systems are frequent and expensive requirements after about fifty thousand miles.

Automotive

Loan Payments	377
Insurance	150
Gasoline	200
Maintenance	10
Subtotal Automotive	737

It appears from these calculations that a car will absorb 34 percent of your net income. We sure are running out of money quickly. We still have $458 left.

Commuting Costs

Finally, we must consider the cost of commuting to work. If you live in the suburbs and have a parking space and if you commute to an institution that has employee parking, then there are no additional costs beyond the costs of gas and maintenance. If, however, you live and work in a densely populated urban area, things change dramatically. You may have to pay for parking in your building. It is not unusual for a parking space to run between $100 and $500 per month in urban areas. If you commute to the city by car, you will have to pay for daily parking. If you're willing to walk, you might be able to pay as little as $10 to $15 a day for parking. A good working number might be around $250 a month. If you are going to live in an urban area and commute by car, then you are probably looking at parking costs in the area of $400 per month.

Subtotal Commuting   400

This represents about 19 percent of your income, and we now have only $58 left. We'll turn our attention from the budget for a while and discuss the options.

The basic choice is between a place to live and a car, although both together are viable. We just need to adjust our perspective.

First, examine your job. If you are going to be working in an urban area with good public transportation, why do you need a car and all its hassles? Use public transportation. I worked in New York City for General Motors during the late 1960s and early 1970s. GM decided to move a large group of employees to Detroit. The biggest problem was that the majority of these employees of the world's largest automotive manufacturer did not have a driver's license. These people had never received a speeding ticket, never changed a tire, never paid automobile insurance, and never had to find a parking place in a full parking lot—imagine the joy that they missed.

Renting a car when you need it can easily solve your problem. A weekend car rental costs about $150. Compare that to the $1,137 it costs you to own a car in the city. You can rent a car every weekend and still be $500 ahead.

If, on the other hand, you live in the suburbs or in a rural area, you clearly need a car to get to work and to play. Examine the amount you pay for rent. Eight hundred dollars is the amount of rent you can expect to pay in an urban area. Some of you may choose to live at home for a while. Many college seniors have enthusiastically assured me that their parents are cool and that this is the best way to save money. I am a parent myself, and I love and respect my children. They are, however, adults with free wills and minds of their own. Often, my mind and their minds are not on the same wavelength, and this is why we are better living apart than under the same roof. Most students who contact me tell me that they moved away from their parents' homes after short periods. You have flown the nest; it's tough to go back.

The bottom line is there are two alternatives:

- Live in an urban area, and take public transportation to work. When you need a car, rent a car.
- Live in a suburban area where the rents are lower, and purchase a car. Hopefully you will have employer-provided parking.

Let's get back to the flow of the budget. Let us examine personal expenses. The first real shock is that there is no meal plan. You have to feed yourself. Let's just work our way through it. Breakfast—I know you don't eat any. I want to offer a piece of advice: you have to have fuel in the engine to make it run well. One of the cheapest ways to feed yourself is to eat a big bowl of sugar-free cereal with milk for breakfast. It also is good for you and costs less than a dollar a day; let's call it $30 a month. If you are a designer coffee addict, add the cost of the double latte mocha grande here. During a twenty-day work month, this habit costs about $50. So breakfast, if you are good to your body, is about $30 a month but can range up to $80 a month.

Next, let's think about lunch. Many institutions have cafeterias that offer nutritional lunches (note that I did not say tasty). These are generally subsidized and are fine sources of the good meals that your mother will inevitably ask if you are eating. They range from about $5 to $10 each. Let's take $8 for an average and multiply it by twenty days; that totals about $160 per month. Several former students who are in the workforce have told me that they have saved money by bringing their lunches from home.

Dinner is tough. In my classes, I use a shared six-pack of beer and a pizza as the standard. Figure $12 for the pizza and $6 for the six-pack; split fifty-fifty, that's $9 a day. That works out to about $270 per month.

It is no longer acceptable to reach into the laundry bag and take out the least dirty item. You're getting paid to be a professional, and you should look and smell like one. Keeping your clothes clean and looking sharp is important to your image and chances for promotion. Figure about $100 here.

Cosmetics and grooming are important. Let's figure about $50.

Credit card payments and student loans depend on the individual; I cannot generalize them, so I will leave them blank. Obviously, they have a dramatic effect on the amount of money that you will have for discretionary activities.

Personal Costs

Breakfast	30
Lunch	160
Dinner	270
Laundry and Dry Cleaning	100
Personal Hygiene, Cosmetics, and Grooming	50
Credit Card Payments	
Student Loan Repayments	
Subtotal Personal Costs	**610**

Scenarios

We'll combine this information into two sample budgets: one for an urban dweller without a car and one for a suburban dweller with a car.

<u>Urban Dweller</u>

Income:

Monthly Salary	$3,000
Withholding (28% of monthly salary)	$ 840
Net Income	**$ 2,160**

Housing

Rent	<u>800</u>
Electricity	<u>35</u>
Heat	<u>30</u>
Water	<u>10</u>
Gas	<u>10</u>
Cable Television	<u>15</u>
Telephone	<u>15</u>
Cellular Telephone	<u>50</u>
Subtotal Housing	**965**

Automotive

Loan Payments	<u>0</u>
Insurance	<u>0</u>
Gasoline	<u>0</u>
Maintenance	<u>0</u>
Subtotal Automotive	<u>**0**</u>
Subtotal Commuting	<u>**100**</u>

Our automotive costs are zero because we don't own a car; however, if you intend to rent frequently, include the cost here. Our commuting costs no longer include parking, but we have figured in the cost of using public transportation to get to work. I used $5 a day for a twenty-day work month in this example.

Personal Costs

Breakfast	<u>30</u>
Lunch	<u>160</u>
Dinner	<u>270</u>

Laundry and Dry Cleaning	100
Personal Hygiene, Cosmetics, and Grooming	50
Credit Card Payments	
Student Loan Repayments	
Subtotal Personal Costs	610
Total Fixed Monthly Costs	1,675

Net Income minus Total Monthly Fixed Costs or Money for Fun and Saving

$495

Living without a car in an urban area gives us a decent chunk of change for a social life.

Suburban resident

Income:

Monthly Salary	$3,000
Withholding (28% of monthly salary)	$ 840
Net Income	**$ 2,160**

Housing

Rent	400
Electricity	35
Heat	30
Water	10
Gas	10
Cable Television	15
Telephone	15
Cellular Telephone	50
Subtotal Housing	565

The assumption here is that you can find an adequate two-bedroom space with a roommate for about half the rent of an urban setting. The assumption is that parking is included.

Automotive

Loan Payments	<u>377</u>
Insurance	<u>150</u>
Gasoline	<u>200</u>
Maintenance	<u>10</u>
Subtotal Automotive	<u>737</u>
Subtotal Commuting	<u>0</u>

Personal Costs

Breakfast	30
Lunch	160
Dinner	270
Laundry and Dry Cleaning	100
Personal Hygiene, Cosmetics, and Grooming	50
Credit Card Payments	
Student Loan Repayments	
Subtotal Personal Costs	<u>610</u>
Total Fixed Monthly Costs	<u>1,675</u>

Net Income minus Total Monthly Fixed Costs or Money for Fun and Saving

$248

At least two things should be clear from this exercise. First, $36,000 a year is an adequate salary on which to live, but one needs to be a capable financial steward. Second, you are not going to be able to have everything that you want from the beginning.

One final thought: after you have been working at your institution for six months, you are going to be faced with deciding whether you want to participate in some kind of tax-qualified retirement program. You're in your twenties and will probably be working for forty-plus years, so why save now?

Let me try to make the case. Most institutions will match your savings, dollar-for-dollar, up to 5 percent of your savings. This is a tremendous return on your money; you will not get this kind of return anywhere else. Let me do the math.

Saving $1 before taxes is the equivalent of forgoing 72 cents of income. (Remember that the government gets 28 percent of your salary before you get your money.) So, you forgo 72 cents, and you end up with your dollar, plus the company's dollar, in a savings account. That is an instant return of 178 percent. (You can calculate this return by dividing $1.28 by $0.72 and then multiplying by one hundred.) I guarantee you that there will be few deals in your lifetime that will yield that kind of return.

If that is not a sufficient reason to save, then you may also want to know that you don't have to wait until you are fifty-nine and a half years old to withdraw the money. Under the current law, you can withdraw the money before this age without paying a penalty for two reasons:

- For a qualified first-time home purchase. ($10,000 lifetime total)

- For qualified higher-education expenses. (Perhaps graduate school?)

If your employer does not match dollar-for-dollar, then tax-deferred saving is not a compelling offer; however, it is still worthy of consideration.

CHAPTER V

Financial Leverage

> Neither a borrower nor a lender be,
> For loan oft loses both itself and friend,
> And borrowing dulls the edge of husbandry.
> William Shakespeare (1564–1616), British poet, *Hamlet* (I. iii)

Financial leverage is a complicated way to say *borrowing money*. It is a very important concept to understand. Let us begin to examine this concept from the lender's point of view.

All financial institutions traffic in money. Their goal is to borrow money at a low cost and then lend it at a higher cost. They consider many things when lending their money, but two of the most important are the following:

- **The reputation of the borrower.**

- **The underlying collateral available to the lender.** Collateral is something that the bank can repossess and sell if the loan is not paid, such as a television, a car, or a home or condominium.

Simply put, on a nationwide scale, lenders operate as follows:

1. Each lending institution establishes its own cost of money. A surrogate for what the bank's money cost might be is the Federal Reserve's discount rate. In March 2007, it stood at 5.25 percent.

2. Each lending institution needs to cover its cost of doing business by considering salaries, business expenses, and profit expectation in order to determine a base interest rate. A good surrogate for this number would be the prime rate. The prime rate is the interest rate that banks are willing to charge to their most creditworthy customers (usually large, solvent corporations). Again, in March 2007, it stood at 8.25 percent. This basically means that banks needed about 3 percent to cover the cost and profit expectation on a very low-risk loan.

3. Then banks add premiums to the rates to cover their credit risks. The higher the credit risk, the greater the premium, which explains the spread in different types of interest rates.

Financial institutions are prepared to lend you money because they expect to make a profit. The things that interest the banks most about you are your earning power, your net worth, and your available collateral. Let's examine them one by one.

1. We assumed in the previous chapter that you are making $36,000 a year. In 2003, according to the U.S. Census Bureau, the median income for a male in the United States was $40,668 and the median income for a female in the United States was $30,724. The median wage for males (of all ages) with bachelor's degrees was $49,985, and the median wage for females (of all ages) with bachelor's degrees was $30,973. You are interesting to a lending institution because you have great future earning potential. The lending institution would love a piece of your future, and it is willing to lend you money now. This fact alone helps explain the number of credit card offers that regularly clog your mailbox.

2. Net worth is simply a statement of the value of everything you own less your outstanding debts. Every time you apply for a major loan, you are required to prepare a net worth statement. It is pretty easy to prepare a net worth statement on your own. Put a line down the center of a piece of paper, and write down everything that you own and the approxi-

mate current market value of each item. For example, clothing normally has no resale value, electronic items might have a small resale value relative to their original costs, and something like a car might have a significant resale value (but lower than its original cost). Then, write down your debts on the right-hand side. Add up each side, subtract the right-hand total from the left-hand total, and you get your net worth. A typical college student's net worth statement might look like this:

Assets		Liabilities	
Bank Accounts	500	Credit Card Debt	1,000
Cash	20	Cell Phone Debt	75
Stocks, Bonds	0	Unpaid Parking Tickets	300
Jewelry	200	Automobile Loan	6,000
CDs	50		
Stereo	100		
Computer	300		
Automobile	7,500		
TOTAL	8,750	TOTAL	7,375

NET WORTH $1,375

This says to the bank that you are solvent, but the bank does not have much to fall back on if it lends you money and you cannot repay the loan. Please note that if you have outstanding student loans, then your net worth is probably negative.

3. Finally, let's use the net worth statement above to discuss collateral. The automobile is collateral for the automobile loan. This means that the bank has a lien on the title, and you cannot sell the car until you pay off the loan. The buyer must provide you with a check, which you will deposit in the lending bank. After the check clears, the bank will remove the lien from the loan, and the buyer will be able to register the car in his or her name. The bank will keep the $6,000, and you will get $1,500.

Let us try to draw some conclusions from this investigation. At this point, we have a great deal of earning potential—which is why banks want to lend us money—but we have little or negative net worth. If we want to preserve most of our future earning power for ourselves and if we want to achieve a positive net worth, then we need to use our leverage intelligently.

First, you should understand that a financial institution can learn a lot about you. A bank will often verify your income by checking with your employer. The bank will almost always get a copy of your credit report. You can also get a copy of your credit report; there are many sites on the Web, including http://www.equifax.com, http://www.experian.com, and http://www.transunion.com. It is always a good idea to find out what the bank will know. If there are blemishes on your credit report, try to clear them up, or have an honest explanation for them. The financial institution will want to know about them. The cleaner your credit record, the lower the interest rate.

We'll start looking at financial leverage by examining the current cost of debt that will be available to you during the next ten years or so.

1. **Credit cards.** Credit card debt requires no collateral. The financial institution does not care what you purchase with your card. Oftentimes, we use credit cards for consumable products—such as concert tickets, clothing, or a round of drinks with our friends—which make no contribution to our net worth. The bank is not too concerned, because it has priced its product to include the potential cost of recovering its money. If worse comes to worse, the bank can get a court order to garnish your wages. In this case, your employer will deduct your credit card payments from your paycheck. Yes, financial institutions can and will do that. During the month of March 2007, when the discount rate was 5.25 percent and prime borrowers were paying 8.25 percent, credit card holders were paying

14%.

In other words, banks felt that they need 3 cents on every dollar lent to make a profit, but they want 5.25 more cents per dollar lent to take the risk associated with credit card debt. Credit cards are very expensive credit.

There are a large number of Internet sites that allow you to calculate the amount of time that you will need to pay off your credit cards and the amount of interest that you will pay. The Web site that I prefer is http://www.bankrate.com. In Appendix A, I have provided step-by-step instructions for how to use this site. If you have a computer handy, you may want to follow the calculations in the appendix for the following example.

Let's say that you have run up $1,000 worth of credit card debt, your interest rate is 14 percent, and you are content to pay off the minimum of $25 a month—that's $300 a year. It will take you ten years and three months to pay off the credit card, and, by that time, you will have paid interest in the amount of $666.96 for the $1,000.00 that you borrowed. This of course assumes that you never use the credit card again.

Let me put that in perspective. Every $200 concert ticket you bought actually cost you $333.38. A $100 blouse, which you purchased because it was reduced to $80, actually cost you $133.35. The round of drinks, which you bought for your friends for $150, actually cost you $250.44.

It is probably obvious to all readers why I am so much against the use of credit cards. They are an easy way to slide into very, very expensive debt. You are essentially spending money that you hope to have sometime in the future, mostly for stuff that you don't need today.

There are some solutions. The first is the debit card. A debit card is easy to set up with a local bank. Basically, it works just like a credit card, but it will not let you spend money when your bank account is empty. Once you have a debit card, cut up every credit card that you have. You may be able to get your bank to give you a single loan, at a rate less than 14 percent, to permit you to pay off all your credit card balances. This puts you well on the way to clearing up negative net worth and to creating a reasonable opportunity to use your buying power on something more positive.

2. **The automotive loan.** This is a loan where we will provide collateral in the form of the car that we are buying. The car will depreciate in value while we own it, so it is good collateral for the bank as long as they can cover most of the outstanding loan by selling the car. Thus, the lender will try to get you to provide a significant down payment. The bank is much more comfortable in this situation because if you don't pay back the loan, it will repossess the car. The bank will issue several warnings to you if your account is past due. If you do not make your payments, the bank will get a court order to repossess your car. A tow truck will come to your house or workplace and take your car. The bank will sell it for whatever money they can get (usually for less than the outstanding value of the loan) and then continue to charge you interest and hound you for the balance. Yes, they can—and do—do that!

During the month of March 2007, when the discount rate was 5.25 percent and prime borrowers were paying 8.25 percent, car loans were priced as follows:

Three-year loans: 6.93%
Five-year loans: 6.97%

During this time, interest on a car loan was approximately 7 percentage points less than interest on a credit card loan. It doesn't take a finance major to figure out that a car loan is a better form of financial leverage than credit card debt.

Prior to shopping for a car, you should figure out how much money is reasonable for you to spend on a car. Once again, we can use the services of many Internet Web sites; we will stick with http://www.bankrate.com. In Appendix A, I give step-by-step instructions for using this Web site to work a car loan example.

By assuming a $1,000 down payment, a finance period of five years (sixty months), and an interest rate of 6.97 percent, we calculate that we can buy a car worth $17,344. That's only $2,000 less than we were going to allocate in our initial budget for a car, and we save more than $50 a month.

3. **The home mortgage.** This is a loan for which we will provide collateral—the home we are purchasing. The difference both to us and to the bank is that, unlike cars, real estate, historically, has appreciated in value. The bank expects to be able to recover its money almost all of the time; only very unique, local real estate conditions would preclude this. Nonpayment would trigger a relatively long period of attempts to collect and renegotiate the loan. However, if a loan default is declared by the court, then you could be evicted from your home, which would be sold off, generally at auction. The bank would then pay off the loan, pay the auctioneer, and give you any remaining money. Yes, they can do that!
During the month of March 2007, when the discount rate was 5.25 percent and prime borrowers were paying 8.25 percent, mortgages were priced as follows:

> **Fifteen-year mortgage loans were 5.41%**
> **Thirty-year mortgage loans were 5.68%**

Interest rates on mortgage loans were less than interest rates on car loans and were between 8 and 9 percentage points less than interest rates on credit card loans.

So why bring it up? **Owning your own dwelling is the most significant financial opportunity you will have in your lifetime.**

Let's examine the advantages of buying your own condominium or house. Perhaps the most significant advantage is the psychological comfort that we get by owning the roof over our heads. There are also great financial rewards.

Let me be clear: I do not recommend that you buy real estate right out of college. During the first few years out of college, you require a great deal of flexibility. It is possible that you will change jobs three or more times in the first five years following graduation. Being a renter allows you to take advantage of professional opportunities that may require geographic moves. You also have no idea what you want. It is unlikely that you will live in a dwelling as cheesy as your dorm room or in one as nice as your parents' home. You also do not have the down payment. Wait until you feel professionally stable, have an idea of where and how you would like to live, and have accumulated around $15,000 for a down payment. This should be achievable sometime in your late twenties or early thirties. Remember the retirement savings account that we discussed at the end of Chapter IV; this money could come in handy. You can withdraw $10,000—penalty-free—for the down payment on your first owner-occupied dwelling.

Let's look at the financial side. If you have $15,000 and a good credit history, then the bank will probably lend you enough money to purchase a $150,000 dwelling.

In Appendix A, I show you how to use http://www.bankrate.com to calculate this value. There are many other Internet sites that provide such calculators.

Assuming that we put down our $15,000, the bank will lend us $135,000 for thirty years at 5.68 percent. The calculator tells us that we will have a monthly payment of $781.83, which is less than we are paying for rent in the urban budget scenario.

Hopefully, this is starting to capture your interest, but I have several other pieces of good news. The federal and state governments allow you to deduct the interest expense on your owner-occupied dwelling from your income taxes. We can use the earlier calculation, which we used while discussing contributions to your retirement savings, to reflect the real cost of the mortgage. Early in the mortgage, almost all of your payment goes toward interest; this declines with time until the last year, when the payment is almost all principal. This means that the tax advantages come early in the game. Let's assume that, of the $781.83 you pay the bank each month, $740.00 is interest. At the end of the year, the total interest for the year will be used to reduce your taxable income. When simplified, this means that $740.00 of your gross income will not be taxed, and, thus, the 28 percent that was withheld will be returned to you when you file your taxes. The real mortgage payment, then, is not $781.83 per month but rather $562.91 ($781.83 minus the $740.00 monthly interest times 0.28, your assumed income tax rate).

The next big advantage arrives when you sell your dwelling. My wife and I have owned three owner-occupied dwellings (we call them homes) in our lifetime. We have friends who have owned as many as ten. But, with few exceptions, the homes of everyone we know have gone up in value.

Assume that five years have passed since you purchased your first home, and enough things have changed for you that you want more space. You put your current home on the market, and it sells for (after all sales costs) $210,000. Let's walk through the math on this transaction.

You receive	$210,000.00
You pay off your mortgage	$124,610.58
You now have:	$ 85,389.42

That is 569 percent of the $15,000 that you paid when you purchased your home, and you have lived rent free for five years. What an investment!

Banks usually require 20 percent down payments from second-time home buyers, so you, if you choose to use your stake to purchase a new house, can buy a new house worth about $425,000.

In my view, there is no stronger argument in the world for tearing up your credit cards and accumulating a small amount of capital in order to make some real money on the appreciation of the home in which you will live.

There are two caveats to buying a home. First, if you own a dwelling, you will need to pay real estate taxes, property insurance, and possibly condominium fees. Research these costs in advance, and make provisions for them in your budget. Second, it is not as easy as I make it sound. First, the real estate market does not go up in a straight line; it is cyclical. Thus, some buyers will get caught paying too much and then losing money when they sell. This happens most often to people who are speculating and do not buy a home for the long term.

Finally, real estate is one of the most illiquid investments. This means that it is hard to turn into cash. If you have a savings account and you need cash, you go to the bank and withdraw it. It can take months or, in a depressed real estate market, years to sell a property. Don't put all your eggs into the real estate basket; have a liquid, rainy-day fund to protect you during sudden events such as job loss, illness, or other catastrophe.

CHAPTER VI

Investing .

No good man ever grew rich all at once
Publis Syrus (42 BC), *Maxim 837*

I was a bit hesitant to write this chapter, because there is so much really good investment advice available everywhere. However, there are some life lessons, which my wife and I have learned, that might be valuable to you when handling the financial aspects of your life.

It seems to me that there are several concepts that we need to understand clearly as we talk about investing. These include your time horizon, liquidity, and the concept of risk and reward.

Time Horizon

How long and for what are we saving? There are probably only a handful of events in your life for which you should be setting aside money. Here is a partial list:

- *Rainy days.* A rainy-day fund is basically a financial safety net. Most experts agree that a person should put about six months' worth of expenses into an easy-to-access investment such as a savings account. Based on the budget in Chapter IV, we might want to set aside somewhere between $10,000 and $12,000. This is the cushion that you will turn to when the car breaks down and needs major repairs, when you need a new piece of furniture, or when you lose your job. Once you take something out, you should endeavor to refill the fund as soon as possible. The time horizon for building this fund should be two to five years.

- *Graduate school.* Setting aside separate funds for this may be difficult, but, if you feel a need to get more education, it is a necessity. A great source of graduate school tuition is tuition-refund programs, which many employers offer. These programs require you to work and attend school at the same time, but many people have survived it. It is nice to have a graduate degree and no debt. You set your own time horizon here, but you should determine when you are going to graduate school and then start saving appropriately.

- *The down payment for your first home.* We talked about this in the last two chapters; it is the shrewdest investment you can make. A practical and tax-effective way to save for a down payment is through the tax-deferred retirement program at work. As discussed in the last chapter, you should have saved enough money for a down payment on a home by the time you reach your late twenties or early thirties.

- *Your child's tuition.* It may have cost more than $100,000 for you to get your college education. Once the kiddies come along, you'll need to start planning early for their education. Hopefully, your children's college years are twenty-plus years away.

- *Your retirement.* You are going to work for about forty years, so you have a nice, long time horizon to save for this event.

Liquidity

Liquidity is the measure of the time it takes to turn an investment into cash. Cash under the mattress is the most liquid investment. However, it earns no return. The purchasing power of the cash declines every day with inflation, and it is not secure—if someone finds and takes it, it's gone. A bank account is a very liquid asset. Checking accounts and, sometimes, savings accounts are convertible into cash during business hours, or after hours through an ATM.

Financial instruments, such as stocks and bonds, are somewhat less liquid in that they take several days to sell and "settle." In the case of stocks, the process normally takes three days, and, in the case of bonds, it can be longer. U.S. savings bonds pay less interest but are more liquid because, with proper identification, you can cash them at any post office or bank.

Anyone who has tried to sell a used car of his or her own has experienced the frustration of turning an asset into cash. It can often take weeks or even months to sell a car, and, frequently, it is difficult to get fair value.

Finally, one of the most illiquid assets is real estate. As I discussed in the last chapter, it can take months—sometimes years—to dispose of a house or land. This is the one real drawback of owning a home.

My wife and I have taken a fairly conventional but simple way of ensuring our liquidity. We have our rainy-day fund, about six months of expenses in cash, in an interest-drawing account. We have some stocks and bonds, but, in order to smooth out some of the variations in the bond market, the maturity of our bonds is staggered over ten years. That is to say, about 10 percent of the portfolio matures, or comes due, each year. If we need the money for something like major repairs to the house, we use it. If not, we roll it over to the eleventh year and keep the tiers intact. We are invested in a diversified stock portfolio, which I will discuss later in this chapter. The last thing that we would rely on in a crisis is the equity in our real estate.

Risk and Reward

Finally, there is the concept of risk and reward. We can refer back to the uncertainty matrix and think about it in a different context. Generally speaking, the higher the risk of an investment, the higher the reward. It is easier to understand this concept in the context of the bond market. A bond is a simple instrument. A business or government borrows money, generally in one-thousand-dollar denominations. That business or government agrees to pay the money back at a fixed time in the future, say twenty years. During the twenty years, the purchaser of the bond will be paid interest at a fixed interest rate. In the bond market, there is a range of interest rates that borrowers will pay in order to use your money. There are two risks that lenders take into account: the creditworthiness of the borrower and the length of the loan period. Obviously, due to potential inflation, there is less risk in lending someone money for thirty days as opposed to thirty years. Below, I give some examples.

U.S. Treasury Bills and Bonds: The U.S. government is considered to be one of the lowest-risk borrowers in the world. The reason for this is that they have the power to tax the richest nation in the world. In May 2005, a three-month U.S. treasury bill, a very low-risk investment, would reward you with an annual interest rate of 2.91 percent per year; a twenty-year U.S. treasury bond would reward you at 4.69 percent, a significant difference. The difference in interest rates is explained by the risk associated with when you get your money back: three months in the case of the U.S. treasury bill and twenty years in the case of the U.S. treasury bond.

Corporate bonds: The creditworthiness of bond-issuing companies is rated by several independent rating agencies. They are rated by letter scores; thus, an AAA-rated bond is much better than a BBB-rated bond. In May 2005, I was able to find some bonds rated BBB that yielded 6.2 percent and matured in four years.

The risk, of course, is that these companies will not be able to pay back your principal in four years, and, despite earning a high return for a while, you will not get your money back.

In summary, if you invest $1,000, you can do the following:

- Earn $29.10 a year with little risk, if you invest in three-month treasury bills for a year

- Earn $46.90 a year with some inflation risk, if you invest in twenty-year treasury bonds

- Earn $62 a year with a significant risk that you will not get your $1,000 back

Thus, the higher the risk we are willing to take, the higher the reward we will potentially receive.

Stocks: Owning stock is owning a small piece of a company. Companies sell stock to people in order to raise money so that they can start a business or expand their businesses. People then resell their shares in financial markets such as the New York Stock Exchange. Large companies have huge numbers of shares outstanding. For example, General Electric has about 10 billion shares outstanding, Coca-Cola has 2.4 billion shares outstanding, IBM has about 1.7 billion shares outstanding, and General Motors has around 560 million shares outstanding. So, you can see that if we purchase a hundred shares of one of these companies, we will own a very, very small piece of the total.

Stocks are bought and sold every day. The three major stock exchanges in the United States are the New York Stock Exchange, the American Stock Exchange, and the NASDAQ. Hundreds of millions and, sometimes, billions of shares are bought and sold on these exchanges every working day of the year. Transactions take place through a broker—like Merrill Lynch, Paine Webber, or Charles Schwab—and the brokers charge a fee for executing the trade. The fees are normally lower per share if you purchase a round lot—for most stocks, this means one hundred shares. Once you purchase a stock, you will receive a stock certificate, or you can leave the stock on deposit with your broker. Leaving the stock on deposit makes the investment more liquid, because you can call your broker and sell it any time that the market is open. If you retain the certificate, you need to sign it and mail it to the broker before the broker will sell the stock.

There is an enormous amount of information on stocks. There are a large number of sites on the Internet where you can access information for free; you can also purchase stock recommendations by professional analysts. Three web sites that provide in-depth financial analysis are Yahoo, MSN, and Bloomberg.

The billions of stocks traded each week are sold and purchased by people who expect that they will make money. Professional traders often make money in small increments by sometimes holding a stock for a few hours or days. The buying and selling of stocks should not be attempted by amateurs, and one should be wary of trying to make money in the market in the short run.

The stock market has grown at an average rate of 10 percent a year over the last one hundred years. Because stocks offer a high reward relative to savings accounts and bonds, there must be some risk. The risk is the volatility of the stock market. Let me give you an example. The Dow Jones Industrial Average is an average of some of the strongest and largest companies in the United States. It is an indicator of growth or contraction of stocks. In 1999, the Dow Jones opened the year at 9,184 and climbed to 11,497 by year's end, an increase of 25.2 percent. Many people believed that it was going to climb forever. Those optimists saw the Dow Jones Average fall to 10,786 by the close of the year 2000, and it continued to tumble to 8,341 by the end of 2002. In April 2007, the Dow Jones Industrial Average topped 13,000 for the first time. Stocks are cyclical and change constantly; you need to be comfortable with risk to be an investor in the stock market. If, however, you take a long-term perspective, say several years, and you diversify your portfolio, then you should have a reasonable expectation of higher returns on stocks than on bonds and savings accounts. How do you diversify your account? If you have a large amount of money, you can create a holding of many different companies in different sectors of the economy. A stockbroker can provide advice on how to diversify your portfolio.

A much easier way to diversify is to buy a mutual fund. Mutual fund companies collect funds from a large number of investors and use the funds to purchase stocks of many companies. Each investor owns a piece of the portfolio, in proportion to his or her investment. Professional managers buy and sell the stocks in the portfolio in line with their research and expectations for stock gains. The professional managers take a small fee for administering the mutual fund. There are literally thousands of mutual funds to choose from. Some good research before you invest will lead you to a mutual fund with an investment philosophy that you are comfortable with. Mutual funds rarely grow as quickly as the "hot" stocks, but they also rarely decline as much as individual stocks. Diversification tends to reduce your risk but limit your reward. Morningstar, at www.morningstar.com, is a great place to learn about mutual funds.

With the concepts of a time horizon, liquidity, diversification, and risk/reward, let's think about how we want to build our net worth.

I believe that we should think in the manner represented by an investment pyramid. It might look something like this:

INVESTMENT TRIANGLE

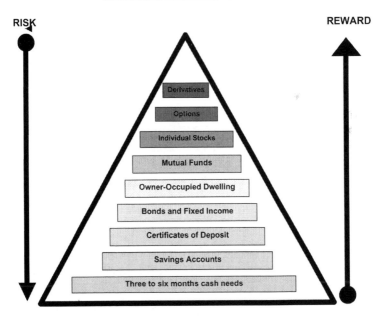

A final word on getting rich quick:

Get Rick Quick

Two favorite sayings come to mind here. The first is "If the offer is too good to be true, it probably is." This has always meant to me that one should be wary of the big deal, the sure thing. Early in my career in New York, a colleague told our office mates that he had a friend who could get color television sets for $100, but we couldn't ask any questions. Color televisions were relatively new at the time and were selling for about $500. About ten of us in the office offered up $100 cash, and our friend gave it to his friend. We never saw the TVs or our money.

A second example is a friend of a friend who invested during the Internet boom of the 1990s. This person found an Internet stock he liked and invested $10,000. The stock grew in value, and he put more of his money into the stock. Eventually, he had about $100,000 invested in this company's stock, and the value of his investment was about $3,000,000. He continued investing, even though the stock started to go down in value, because he was confident that the stock would grow again. Eventually, the bubble burst, and the roughly $250,000 of his family savings that he had invested was worth about $19,000. He failed to get his money out when he could, which leads to my second-favorite saying, "The bulls and the bears always make out; the pigs never do." There are millions of people who study and analyze the stock market every day. Most of them make money in small increments. It is unlikely that anyone is going to outsmart these millions of other investors for long. Thus, anyone who offers you quick riches is someone to steer away from. This is particularly true if it is free advice. Run away from tips like, "My brother-in-law knows somebody, who went to this weather forecaster who said there was going to be a drought in the Midwest—so sell corn futures, short." Like most things you do on your journey, well-thought-out decisions, accompanied by a lot of research and preparation, are likely to yield the best long-term results.

Luck does play a role in this risk/reward formula. So, if you are like the Internet investor in the above example, and you do hit a lucky streak, then be sure to diversify. One rule that I followed when investing during the Internet bubble was that if my money doubled, I would take out my initial stake and put it into a conservative investment. This always felt good to me; it felt like I was playing with the house's money.

The investment with the highest risk/reward ratio legally available is the high-stakes lottery game. Feeling lucky? Buy a few Lotto tickets. It will scratch an itch for a few bucks and might keep you from throwing away hundreds or thousands of dollars on a bad investment.

One final note: no matter how much research you do and no matter how careful you are, there are going to be times when investments in your portfolio are going to go down. Real estate values tumble, stock and bond markets go down as well as up, and interest rates can go up, which drives bond values down. If you are well diversified and have a reasonable time frame, don't sweat it. Move on, and don't be obsessed with money. It is important to handle it prudently, but, in the end, as my brother Bill says, "Money is just a bunch of green fun coupons; let's enjoy."

CHAPTER VII

Career Development at Work

Every company has two organizational structures: The formal one is written on the charts; the other is the everyday relationship of the men and women in the organization.
Harold S. Geneen and Alvin Moscow, *Managing,* Doubleday, 1984

Corporate risk takers are very much like entrepreneurs. They take personal risks to make new ideas happen
Gifford Pinchot III, *Intrapreneuring,* Harper & Row, 1985

Life is an oral pop quiz.
Chuck Matzell, a friend

For the next forty years or so, your life will incorporate work. It will be the longest of the three major phases of your journey. The growing up and education stages lasted some twenty-plus years. You'll have forty-plus years of work, followed by some well-earned leisure, which we call retirement. It seems to me that there are some things that I can share about work that will be helpful in guiding you in the journey. A career is more like a marathon than a sprint. Conserve energy, focus on your goals, and don't get distracted by the small aches and pains that come with forty years on the job.

Let's start with career management. One of the keys to success and happiness in a job is for you to understand that you are responsible for your career. This may sound obvious, but, in my lifetime, I have seen hundreds of people waiting for things to happen to them or wondering, often bitterly, why they have been left behind. Just as you are responsible for your job search, you are also responsible for setting goals and setting the criteria for success in your career. I cannot tell you the number of times in my career when I conducted a performance review with a poorly performing subordinate who would conclude the interview by rationalizing, "It's okay; the company will take care of me." It struck me, after hearing this many times, that it was an uninformed statement. In the first place, institutions are inanimate; they are not capable of thought, of compassion, or of taking care of anyone. An institution is basically a collection of physical assets being managed by people. The skills of the people managing the assets determine the success of the institution and the employment security of the employees. People who do not understand this simple fact abdicate any responsibility for their own careers; they put themselves in the red zone of the uncertainty matrix for most of their lives. Many of the people who told me that the company would take care of them were the first to be laid off when the company got into trouble.

I roughly estimate that each graduating college senior has about $500,000 invested in him or her. Your parents spent that money while raising you, providing you with shelter and food, catering to your entertainment whims, and educating you. It is your responsibility to manage this large asset and earn a reasonable return on the investment; you can do that only by being proactive.

First, pause and consider your long-term goals. They will probably revolve around the three things we discussed in Chapter I: helping others (which includes investing time into your family), power, and money. For most of us, these things are just sketchy concepts, and, often, we cannot articulate them precisely. However, as life goes along, we will need to balance one against the other.

As you get older, there is a unique relationship between time and money. Today, you have a good deal of time to call your own—some of you even use it to study—and very little money, as we have seen in the preceding chapters. As your responsibilities and your income increase, the situation will reverse itself: you will have a significant amount of "money for fun and saving," as we called it in Chapter IV, but you will be squeezed for time. Often, people in their late forties and fifties have sufficient money, which they start to trade for more time. For example, instead of driving to Florida for a visit to Disney World with the family, everyone flies there, saving time and effort. The point, however, is that the pursuit of money often goes too far; you can find yourself earning money that you will never be able to spend. As desirable as this seems today, watch yourself, and try to keep equilibrium in your life.

My assumption is that you are ambitious and would like to have as much satisfaction as you can at this point in your life from helping people, having power, and earning money. After college graduation, you are independent and unfettered, free to take some risks, and ready to reach for the sky. Let me suggest some things that may be relevant to your first years on the job.

Why Were You Hired?

You need to understand why you were hired. You were not hired because you are smart, because of what you learned in sixteen years of school, or because you have a charming personality. You were hired because you have proven that you have the capacity to learn. Most institutions, with the exception of elementary and secondary schools, do not expect you to be productive for some time. Therefore, job number one is to learn as much as you can about the department, institution, and industry. Do not restrict yourself to the internal training that you receive; learn everything that you can from outside sources. Consider this to be the most challenging course that you have ever taken and immerse yourself into learning all that you can about your institution. Listen to your peers and, particularly, to the old-timers; this is the fastest way to get up to speed.

How Will People Judge You?

The second thing that you need to understand is that people are judging you on three criteria: your capacity to work, your ability to communicate, and your ability to fit into the culture of the institution.

Capacity to Work

Sooner or later, someone will ask you to do something: research a topic, write a memo, or examine a new technique. Take on this task as if your career depends on it—it does. Do as thorough and complete a job as you can. Present your conclusions in a concise summary form, and then include as much detailed backup information as is relevant. Your summary will indicate your respect for the reader's time, and your backup will indicate your respect for the reader's intellect. Somebody is going to say to himself or herself, "This kid is a worker! Let's give this kid more to do." Excel in every assignment you are given. This way, you are increasing your value to your department and to the institution and influencing the outcome of your career. Ignore those coworkers who say, "Hey, don't work so hard—you're making us all look bad." You will soon be their boss.

Learn to Speak Well

It has been my observation that the current generation of students is made up of poor oral communicators. I was discussing this with a friend and describing how difficult it was to convince students that clear, well-thought-out dialogue was one of the keys to a successful career. Chuck Matzell said, "Tell them life is an oral pop quiz."

Here are some suggestions to improving the way you communicate orally:

- Take a public speaking course. Even if you have graduated, learning how to project your voice and form your words will significantly improve your public persona.

- Open your mouth when you speak. Many of my students try to say words without moving their lips. Perhaps it's cool in college, but it will reflect poorly on you in the outside world.

- Use all of your vocabulary. Conversations filled with words and phrases like "yeah," "awesome," and "I don't know" are fine with your friends, but they indicate a lazy mental attitude.

- Speak loudly enough for your audience to hear you. Project your voice. As you gain experience, use tonal changes to make your point.

- Establish and maintain eye contact.

- Be sure that your brain is connected to your mouth before you speak. Try to organize a response before you begin talking. State your point, support your point, and summarize.

- Adopt an enthusiastic, can-do attitude in your conversation.

Institutional Culture

The culture of the institution is also important. Institutions operate across a wide range of cultures, and each culture has its own unwritten rules. In some organizations, the senior managers access all levels of their organizations and have their hands in everything, but, in others, the senior management may appear only on formal occasions and speak to their employees as a group. An employee should behave differently in each culture. Some organizations rely on a few people to make most of the decisions, others rely on committees, and yet others delegate decision making to employees throughout the organization. One way to learn a great deal about a company's culture is to listen to stories and legends that employees freely share with you. Just as in early tribal behavior, norms of behavior are passed on through stories. Many people will share snippets of past experiences within the company that will provide examples of both acceptable and unacceptable cultural behavior.

Here are a couple of incidents that I remember from my career. During my first performance review at General Motors, my supervisor told me a story about an employee who arrived at work about a half an hour before starting time and quickly moved up the ladder. I got the message and started coming to work early. A few weeks later, I was sitting at my desk when, at about 7:30 one morning, a manager four levels above me came into my office, a large space that I shared with about thirty other people. Because I was the only one there, he asked me for some help, which I gladly gave him. Later that afternoon, my supervisor said to me, "I told you if you came in early it would pay off; you're now a candidate for a two-year leadership training program."

Another example comes from later in my career while I was working for another large company. We went on an executive retreat, and the invitation had indicated that casual dress was appropriate. I was in my late thirties, and casual to me was jeans and a T-shirt. I showed up the first afternoon and everyone was wearing slacks, button-down dress shirts open at the collar, and blue blazers with brass buttons. I skipped the next morning session and bought myself an outfit that conformed to the company's view of casual.

The legends that your coworkers discuss will also demonstrate unacceptable behavior. "So-and-so was fired because he got caught using the company credit card while filling his wife's car up with gas. So-and-so is going nowhere because she had too many drinks at the office party and was walking around with a lampshade on her head." Listen, observe, and learn.

Many organizations have employee manuals that capture some of the large issues related to the company's culture. The important thing is to be aware of the culture and try to adapt to it. If you are uncomfortable with the culture of the institution, you just found your first reason to manage your career and look for a new job. In your next set of job interviews, you will be more aware of the cultural aspects of the institution that you are considering.

What Is the Management Looking For?

When I was trying to spot young talent, I looked for the following characteristics:

- A positive attitude—people that approach a challenge with a positive attitude and are able to see the upside of a situation
- Honesty—the ability to tell it like it is without embellishment
- Accountability—the ability to admit a mistake quickly and openly without excuses
- Confidence—the ability to move forward on an assignment and make decisions without checking in all the time
- Thoroughness—the ability to bring assignments to conclusions
- Flexibility—the willingness to do what it takes to get a job done correctly
- Thoughtfulness—the ability to keep peers and supervisors informed so that they are not surprised by information
- Leadership—the ability to organize and direct people toward a common goal

Obviously, I did not find all these traits in very many people. As a manager, I included people who possessed some of these characteristics on my lists for promotion, training, and advancement.

Manage the Relationship with Your Boss

Your relationships with your manager and with the hierarchy that supervises your manager are important. Many young, egocentric professionals believe that their managers and the rest of the hierarchy think about them regularly. This is simply not true. Most people in supervisory positions are time constrained; they are far busier than you can imagine. Most are proactively managing their own careers and are far more preoccupied with their peer group and with the hierarchy than they are with their subordinates. They have taken responsibility for their own careers and will respect someone who is doing the same. So, how often do managers think about their subordinates as individuals? They think of you, perhaps, once a year when they conduct the annual performance review. In this environment, how do you manage your own career?

First, set realistic goals for yourself. After you have been at an institution for six months to a year, you should have a clear picture of career opportunities. What seem to be logical career paths? What do the criteria for promotion seem to be? Where would you ultimately like to go in this organization, and what is the next step to getting there? You can answer these questions by observing the movement in the organization. Organizations change regularly, sometimes by design (such as reorganization) and sometimes by chance (such as when a key player leaves the institution). What happens when these events occur, who are the key players, and what are the characteristics of the people who get ahead?

Define a goal for yourself: I want to move away from teaching into administration, I want to become a lieutenant on the police force, I want to head the engineering task force on quality control, I want to become an audit supervisor, I want to be a sales manager, or I want to supervise the payroll department. Then, research the key qualifications for the job. For example, to be a police lieutenant, you need certain experience and you must pass a test. Start working toward passing the test. To be a sales manager, you need experience as a salesperson; if you are not out on the road now, get transferred to a sales position. Most importantly, you need to openly discuss your goal with your manager. This is important for two reasons. First, speaking with your manager is the first step to realizing your goals. Until you make your interests known, your manager can only guess your goals. Basically, discussing your career goals with your supervisor pulls you out of the red zone of uncertainty and puts you into the orange zone. Second, your supervisor, who has in-depth knowledge of the institution, can help you define realistic and achievable goals. When I returned to General Motors after my military service, my goal was to be transferred to a job in one of

General Motors' international subsidiaries. During my six-month review, I discussed this goal with my manager. For about an hour, he coached me on the steps necessary for achieving that goal. Within weeks of our discussion, he sponsored me for a special internal training program aimed at preparing candidates for overseas assignments. Several years later, General Motors sent me to Switzerland to work in a marketing position in its Swiss subsidiary. If I had not held the conversation with my first manager during my six-month performance review, I am not sure that I would have achieved my goal.

Internal Networking

Letting your manager know what you want is the first step to managing your career proactively. The next step is to develop a network throughout the organization. There are two ways to do this when you first join an organization. The first way is to develop relationships with mentors. Many organizations have formal mentor programs. Get involved as soon as possible, and gather advice from your mentors as you begin to form and articulate your goals. Mentors normally volunteer to perform this task. They are looking to provide guidance, and they know a great deal about the organization's drawbacks and opportunities. When meeting with a mentor, be prepared and time efficient. Remember that mentors are taking time away from their jobs to help you, so don't be a time hog. It is up to you to communicate and stay in touch with your mentor; a phone call once a month will help to keep your mentor involved and interested in your progress.

The other way to develop your internal network is to serve on task forces and committees. Here, you will meet people from other disciplines and begin to understand cross-departmental issues. Most importantly, you should try to acquire a familiar contact from another department. This will enable you to get information on problems that are beyond the scope of your immediate area of influence. One of my students took a job in the suburban branch of a large bank. She was asked to serve as a representative of the United Way campaign for her department. During the course of the year, she attended numerous committee meetings at the bank's headquarters. It came as a complete surprise to her when someone she worked with on the committee offered her a significant promotion and an opportunity to move to the headquarters. Obviously, she impressed a number of people with the quality of her work on the campaign.

Power

No discussion of building organizational understanding would be complete without talking about power and leadership. Power is a very elusive thing—it is hard to acquire, difficult to describe, and difficult to use effectively. However, power is the force that shapes the way that events unfold within an organization.

Political scientists seem to have an excellent grip on power. I often advise my business students to take Political Science 101 to learn how political scientists identify and categorize power.

Every institution attempts to allocate power throughout the hierarchy. In the United States, we have the Constitution, which clearly delineates and allocates power to three separate institutions—the Congress, the presidency, and the judicial branch of government. Most institutions have formal documents that allocate power and decision-making authority. An institution commonly uses an organization chart to illustrate the flow of authority and power throughout the organization. These charts can help you, a new employee, identify the important people in the organization and understand how power flows through the organization. The charts, however, rarely represent the true power structure of the organization or where power and decision making are concentrated.

A college graduate entering an organization has almost no formal or informal power. Formal power, to me, is the authority that is allocated to a person as a result of his or her position in the organizational structure. Institutions have extensive manuals regarding the allocation of power. These manuals clearly spell out such items as who has the authority to make financial decisions, who is allowed to make hiring and firing decisions, and who is allowed to speak publicly for the institution. As you climb the ladder, you will acquire more and more allocated power.

Informal power is more difficult to identify and far more important than formal power in any organization. A person or a coalition of people acquires informal power because of the force of their personalities, because of the knowledge they possess, or because of their immediate importance to the organization. As you observe the organization, attend meetings, and watch major changes occur within the organization, you will find that certain people have more influence on events than others. Quickly, you will also observe that the influence of the shakers and movers does not necessarily correspond to their positions in the hierarchy. Furthermore, as you watch things evolve over time, you will see the power quotient of individuals rise and fall. Informal power is a potent fuel that pushes the organization and, when correctly managed and focused, can create positive change and impetus for the organization. When incorrectly managed, it will often lead to dissension and strategic mistakes. Why is this important to you? To effectively manage your career, you need to understand informal power and eventually to acquire it.

The first piece of advice that I have about power, particularly about informal power, is to observe it for years before you try to get involved. I want to offer a brief story. A student who was working full-time came to me with a problem. He had recently assumed supervisory responsibility for the computer operations on the night shift. As such, he was required to attend a regular, weekly staff meeting. The meetings were uneventful for several weeks. Then, one week, his boss was unable to attend the meeting. During this meeting, the supervisor of day shift computer operations degraded him in front of his colleagues and implied that the night operation was running poorly. This student wanted me to help him plan a counterattack, which he would launch at the next meeting. Before doing that, I suggested that he talk to his manager, who had been absent from the meeting. He did, and he reported back to me that his manager said that she would take care of things. He was upset and wanted vengeance. I counseled him to wait and helped him understand that his manager had a great deal of informal power. She was likely to be more effective than he would be in this situation. Two weeks later, my student came to class and proudly told me that the supervisor of the day shift had been demoted. I was particularly pleased to see my student show restraint. Not only did he achieve the vindication he sought, but also his manager, by supporting him with her power, provided him with some informal power. People will think twice before messing with him in the future.

Some of the things that I've learned about informal power over the years are as follows:

- No matter what level you are at within an organization, you have no informal power if you are a new employee. Try to remain on the sidelines as long as possible.

- If you are new to an organization, people will test your power. Maintain appropriate boundaries, but try to avoid open conflict until you have accumulated and consolidated your power.

- If you intend to exercise informal power, apply it gradually. Often, it does not take much to influence people to behave the way you would like.

- In a power struggle, be as rational as possible and assess your chances of succeeding. A gracious retreat from a situation is always preferable to an embarrassing defeat. The exception to this rule is that you should never retreat when you are defending a moral or ethical standard.

- Reverse the old sayings "Be a good loser" and "Be a good winner." As soon as you have achieved victory, cease the application of power and extend a hand to the opposition. Be gracious in victory and rational in defeat. There is little value in wasting power to "get even." There will be new conflicts with different people, and you need to conserve your resources for those conflicts. Remember, your journey is a marathon, not a sprint.

- The more power you have, the less you need. In fact, the effect you have when you have power can sometimes be frightening. Pete Estes, the president of General Motors in the 1970s, shared the following story with me. Pete was an engineer and loved automobiles. In the 1970s, GM introduced disc brakes on the front two wheels of its cars but retained drum brakes on the rear two wheels. Pete attended a high-level engineering meeting and asked what the effect would be if disc brakes were installed on all four wheels. He got some informal feedback at the meeting and was satisfied to let the program continue as established. Six months later, long after he had forgotten the question, he told me that he received a five-hundred-page study that detailed the engineering, financial, and marketing implications of putting disc brakes on all four wheels. He was shocked by the large amount of time and money that had been devoted to the study, which was written because people had misinterpreted his casual request for information as a mandate to allocate resources.

Power—it exists, you need to understand it, you need to acquire it, and you need to use it carefully.

Leadership

Leadership is a concept that you are familiar with and exposed to every day. The groups that you hang out with, the clubs in which you participate, and the teams that you play with all have leaders. Sometimes, depending on the circumstances, the leaders change. In your group, when you get into a threatening situation, the alpha male might take control. If you are in a situation that calls for strategy and cunning, a thinking person might take over. When you are in a crisis, the person with poise and control might take over. In your group, you have a good, unspoken understanding of each member's skills and are willing to follow them when their skill set is demanded. It is likely that you can think of circumstances where you were called upon to demonstrate your leadership.

Organizational behaviorists study leadership and can offer useful concepts and insights. First, there is a debate over whether leadership is a natural talent or whether it can be taught. My own opinion is that it is a bit of both. The experts have also described different types of leadership behavior. Generally there is a leadership spectrum, with authoritarian leaders at one extreme and democratic leaders at the other extreme.

An example of an authoritarian leader is a military petty officer. Through exhaustive conditioning of their troops, military petty officers train every soldier to obey their commands instantly. The soldiers respect and trust the judgment of their leaders and understand that their lives depend on the instantaneous response to their leaders' commands.

On the other end of the spectrum, we have the democratic leader. An example of this type of leader might be the president of the local school board. This person leads a group of well-educated, highly motivated volunteers. The president has no leverage over the members of the organization. The president cannot fire anyone, cannot reduce anyone's pay, and cannot demote anyone. Each of the members of the organization has different viewpoints and agendas. The parent of a talented student-athlete is anxious to see the school put more money into athletics, the parent of an intellectually gifted child in junior high school wants more money to go toward the purchase of computers and science materials, and the parents of young children in elementary school want better reading and mathematics programs. Hours of discussion and compromise are necessary to reach decisions regarding the allocation of the limited financial resources of the school district and to get enough votes to pass the budget.

Imagine the disasters that could occur if the time-consuming decision-making system of the school board were used in a battle or if the hard-driving master sergeant tried to lead the school board. Different situations call for different leadership styles. In your real-world endeavors, you will have many opportunities to observe leaders before you are placed in a leadership situation. Use the autocratic–democratic spectrum to classify these leaders, and observe the strengths or weaknesses that each style brings to a given situation. Then, imagine what you might do in a similar situation.

The essence of leadership is this: the people you wish to lead must be willing to follow you. A good leader creates an environment in which people are willing to follow. There are a number of observations I have made regarding leadership.

First, you do not have to be liked to be a leader; you need to be trusted and respected. No one likes the authoritarian sergeant, because all he does is yell; no one likes the president of the school board, because it takes her so long to make a decision. It takes time and a great deal of personal effort to earn trust and respect. Key aspects of earning trust and respect are as follows:

- *Be self-confident.* Leaders need to be in control and have the ability to arrive at timely decisions.

- *Be honest and forthright in communications.* Leaders deliver both good and bad news promptly and honestly. They do not try to spin information for others' benefit. They treat people as mature adults and take time to answer questions and deal with concerns while removing as much uncertainty as possible from the environment.

- *Keep your word.* When you commit to doing something, you execute until the situation gets out of your control. When this happens, you inform people that you are no longer capable of delivering your word, and you move with them to the next desirable course of action.

- *Have a consistent vision, and communicate it regularly.* One of my mentors, who was an excellent leader, once told me that people start to buy into your vision only after you have become bored repeating it. You must have consistency and constancy in your communications. It takes people some time to catch on to what you are trying to accomplish. A corollary of this idea is that you should not change your vision too often; this creates uncertainty and leads to mistrust.

- *Be able to move forward with the wind in your face.* Stick to your guns, be true to your vision, compete for resources, and be courageous. People want to follow leaders who have the strength to move forward with conviction.

- *Listen, listen, and listen.* As you assume increasing leadership responsibility, you will be bombarded with advice and criticism. Take it all in, but decide for yourself. When you make a decision, be clear about your expectations and enumerate both the path to the goals and the reason for your decision. After making a decision, express your appreciation to those whose ideas you did not select.

- *Maintain a distance from the people you are trying to lead.* This does not mean that you should be aloof or arrogant; it means that you cannot be "one of the guys" and also be a leader. It is more desirable to socialize with your peers than with your subordinates.

- *Never shoot the messenger.* One of the most important aspects of leadership is how you behave when you receive information. If you are critical of people who bring you bad news and commend people who give you good news, then people will bring you only good news. This can be a critical error, because an important role of a leader is to deal with setbacks. Thus, you must encourage people to come forward with problems as quickly and openly as possible. It takes some practice and discipline to react equally to bad and good news.

- *Absorb the criticism; share the praise.* Good leaders try to absorb criticism directed at the group, and they share the praise that comes to the group.

- *Deal aggressively with malcontents.* There will always be some people who do not want to follow you; this is particularly true when you assume leadership of a new group. People who are unhappy or resentful of your leadership will quickly become apparent. Work with these people one-on-one in order to understand and deal with their issues. Give the individuals some time to come around, but if you don't make progress, transfer or dismiss them from your group. It is true that one rotten apple can spoil the barrel.

Most companies will offer leadership training programs prior to an employee's assumption of a leadership role. These programs are worthwhile, and they will help you understand the leadership environment in the company and your legal obligations as a leader.

Loyalty

A quick word here about loyalty. You may recall that, at the beginning of this chapter, I suggested that an institution is a collection of assets with no ability to think or to care. So why would anyone be loyal to an institution? I cannot think of a good reason. You do owe a certain amount of loyalty to your coworkers and managers, particularly if they have treated you well and have dealt with you in an honest, open fashion. That loyalty goes only so far, because they cannot offer or guarantee your security. Due to constant changes in budgets, institutional objectives, and levels of productivity and automation, no one is guaranteed a job in today's world. Businesses, educational institutions, and governmental institutions are constantly readjusting their headcounts to meet current conditions. The bottom line is that you can easily become expendable no matter how well you perform, how important you think you are to your institution, or how much your managers like you. If it is the institution's prerogative to drop you whenever it suits them, then it is also your prerogative to move to another institution if you find a better opportunity. Thus, my advice concerning loyalty in the workplace is this: possess the traits enumerated above, but always be on the lookout for a better, more attractive opportunity.

One of the great facts of job hunting is that it is much easier to find a job when you have a job. The two main reasons for this are as follows:

- You are much more confident and capable in an interview if you currently have a job. You go into the interview knowing that you are going back to work and not going home simply to sit by the phone and wait for somebody to call. I have changed jobs both ways—after being laid off and moving from one job to another. I learned the hard way that I was much more convincing in the interview when I was relaxed and felt that I didn't need to convince this interviewer to give me a job because I needed a job.

- The hiring institution sees you in a much more positive light. Despite the fact that you may have been laid off with thousands of other people, you are slightly damaged goods in the eyes of the interviewer. Interviewing and landing someone who has a job is a much more exciting and challenging task for an interviewer and for an institution.

In the next chapter, we will deal with managing your career in the external environment.

CHAPTER VIII

Career Development Outside of Work

God helps them that help themselves.
Benjamin Franklin (1706–90), *Maxims,* prefixed to *Poor Richard's Almanac* (1757)

The next important step in your journey is to begin to establish contacts outside of your organization. The current thinking in the business community is that people who begin their careers in the first decade of the new millennium will have between ten and fifteen employers during their forty-year careers. You likely will change jobs frequently in your early career and then less frequently as you climb the ladder, when fewer opportunities for change are available. It is essential to begin to build a network of contacts outside of your institution.

To begin building a network, join and attend meetings of the professional societies related to your specialty. There are a large number of such groups in the United States, and a quick search on the Internet will yield more groups than you can possibly join. Selecting and then attending meetings of one or several of these groups will provide you with great insight into your profession and your industry. Most importantly, you will learn about the growth opportunities within your specialty. Many of these groups actually operate Internet sites on which member institutions can post job openings. Visiting these Web sites is a great way to keep track of opportunities and pay ranges for your profession.

The next and most obvious place for finding future opportunities is the want ad section of the newspaper. The major difference between answering a want ad and posting your résumé on an Internet job site is the level of confidentiality. Your employer may discover that you are searching for a new job if your résumé is posted on the Internet; when discretion is required, it is better to answer a want ad. Using the Internet to e-mail your résumé directly to employers' Web sites and searching the want ads are effective ways of finding a new job, particularly in professions where licensing and other credentials are important.

There are three groups of middlemen who bring job seekers and employers together. First, there are temporary agencies. These businesses fill short-term employment needs, generally for businesses. They are known as temporary employment agencies. Historically, these agencies filled mostly clerical jobs, but the range of employees that they place has increased greatly in recent years. There are two principal reasons for their growth. The first is the high cost of benefits. Businesses do not have to pay benefit costs for temporary workers. The second reason is that many businesses like the "try before you buy" feature of temporary workers. A business can bring in temporary workers and measure their worth before putting them on the payroll. Many of my students who did not find permanent jobs after graduation have found temporary work to be an effective way to gain a permanent position.

The next groups of businesses that bring job seekers and employers together are called employment agencies. Employment agencies generally operate in the lower and middle levels of management. They are usually licensed by the state. Many will be specialized in certain areas such as accounting, sales, information technology, or clerical work. The larger agencies will have multiple specialties under one roof. All of the good employment agencies derive their incomes from fees paid by the employers. One should be wary of agencies that require a fee from the job seeker. Employment agencies can be valuable as you begin to build your career.

Finally, there are executive search firms, whose employees are referred to as "recruiters" or "headhunters." They recruit candidates for senior positions within organizations. Executive search firms are always paid by the employer and can take several months to thoroughly research candidates and present them to a potential employer. As one progresses in a business career, it is important to develop contacts within search firms. Many executive recruiters have Web sites where you can register and post your résumé. They then use these databases to scan for desirable characteristics when they are seeking a candidate for a particular job opening. Generally, they prefer to recruit people who are currently employed, so it is wise to keep your contacts and résumé current. *Consultant News,* the newsletter for this industry, publishes a list of executive recruiters. You can obtain it for a fee by contacting them at 603-585-2200 or on the Web at http://www.kennedyinfo.com. When recruiters contact you, they often open the conversation by identifying themselves, giving you a brief sketch of the job search that they are conducting, and asking if you know anyone who might be interested. They really want to know if *you* are interested. If you decline or show no interest, they will, like good networkers, ask if you know anyone who might be interested.

Finally, you should work on improving your professional skills. The best way to do this is to get more education. Increasingly, this may require that you attend school while you are working. This often puts a big dent in your social life but pays major dividends, both in terms of lifetime income and in terms of advancement.

CHAPTER IX

Supervision

As soon as the boss decides he wants his workers to do something,
he has two problems: making them do it and monitoring what
they do.
Robert Krulwich, "Motivating the Help," *New York Times*, July 4, 1982

The person who knows "how" will always have a job. The person
who knows "why" will always be his boss.
Diane Ravitch, commencement address at Reed College (Portland,
Oregon), reprinted in *Time*, June 17, 1985

For many of my readers, a major step in your careers will occur
when you become managers. This does not mean that you will automatically become a leader. Upon joining a management team, you
will be assigned physical and human resources, as well as a budget.
Your responsibility will be to use these resources as efficiently as
possible to meet and exceed organizational goals. At this point, you
will add "managing" to your "doing" and "learning" skills.

It is likely that you will receive some management training
before you assume supervisory responsibilities. The training will
cover topics including human relations, your company's policies,
and your legal responsibilities as a supervisor. This information will
be helpful but will not totally prepare you for your new job.

Physical Resources

Physical resources are the tangible assets assigned to you. Included in this category are buildings, equipment, furnishings, and other items with physical lives longer than a year. In some industries, such as manufacturing, these resources will be vital to the success of the group. In other industries, the physical resources are less critical to performing the mission but may be vital to the efficiency of the group. For example, the efficiency of your group may depend on the age and capacity of the computers, software, and network that your employees use daily.

A key to effectively managing physical resources is to understand how they are procured. Most organizations have two budget levels: a capital budget and an operating budget. Both get a great deal of scrutiny, and the approval process for each budget is one of the key events that occur every year. In most organizations, the amount of money that is available for capital improvements is limited, and there are many competing proposals throughout the organization for the limited budget. Thus, it is important for the individual manager to identify needs for capital improvement well in advance of expected implementation. After identifying those needs, it is necessary to make your case. Often, there is a specific form to use when requesting capital improvements. The forms normally require both a strategic justification and a financial justification. Capital expenditures that attract the senior management's attention are those that offer significant returns by providing increased productivity, significant efficiencies, or major cost savings. The creation of a capital improvement request, therefore, requires forward planning, a high degree of preparation, and strong justification. Good managers are aware of their groups' capital needs, have a priority list, and have several capital requests in the system. The finance department, which has control over these expenditures, can be very helpful in preparing successful requests—enlist its help, if possible.

Human Resources

One of the promises that I made to myself in business school was that I would be a good boss. My view of a good boss at the time was someone who provided enlightened guidance to a group of highly motivated, happy workers. Our group was going to be the most productive, most efficient, and most highly motivated unit in the organization.

During the first years of my career (when I was just a worker bee), I began to realize that all bosses were idiots. After all, during conversations with my peers, we would complain regularly about our bosses. Most of you can relate to this; you surely have had conversations about the weaknesses of your bosses. If management is incompetent, then it must be very easy to be a boss.

Then, I was given my first supervisory assignment. What a shock. I recall thinking two things at the time. First, I wondered why I was selected to supervise this group. All of my subordinates were older than I was and had more experience with the company. How was I going to tell them anything? Second, instead of having a group of dynamic people who were hungry for guidance from an enlightened manager, I had a group of relatively discontent employees who were uninterested in anything but getting through the day. The bubble burst on the first day. Over the next few days, I found out that it was lonely at the top. Of course, I was far from the top, but, even on the first rung of the supervisory ladder, the social aspect of the job had changed. Basically, I was now the target of the group's criticism (the idiot).

The management of human resources is the most difficult task that you will be assigned in your organization. Perhaps some of my life experiences will provide you with some guidelines for this task.

First, let us make a clear distinction between management and leadership. Good managers need to be leaders, but they do not need to be great leaders. Good leaders often do not make good managers. We discussed leadership characteristics in Chapter VII. Strong leaders are visionaries with the ability to earn the trust and respect of their followers in order to execute their visions. They are often willing to sacrifice the interests of their followers to achieve their visions. Managers, on the other hand, have more clearly defined goals and resources. The task of a manager is to focus the resources at hand to achieve goals in the most efficient fashion. The task that you have been given as a boss is essentially a management task. If you also demonstrate leadership in this task, it is likely to accelerate the progression of your career.

Let us next discuss what it means to be a good manager. First, you must understand the mission and goals for your group. You can establish this understanding through dialogue with your boss. Ask the following questions: What is the mission of my group? What are the short-term and long-term goals? How will the progress of my group be measured? What discretionary authority do I have? Can I hire and fire people? (Probably not.) Can I give discretionary incentives such as bonuses or salary increases? (Probably not.) If at all possible, you should have clear answers to these questions before you even meet your new group.

First impressions are important. Your introduction to your group is an important step in setting the tone for your management tenure and in establishing your management style. The introduction may be as informal as your boss walking you around, introducing you to seven or eight people, and telling them that you're the new boss. Or, you may be introduced in a formal meeting where several levels of management and the former supervisor are present. You may even have a transition period in which the old manager sticks around to orient you to the job. This method is undoubtedly the most awkward. The subordinates are uncertain about who is in charge, the old supervisor is anxious to get on with his or her new job, and you are in an awkward position.

In any case, there will come a day when you are alone with your new subordinates. My first objective always was to reduce the amount of uncertainty. A new boss almost automatically puts all the subordinates into the red zone of the uncertainty chart. You are an unknown decision maker in their lives, and you will make important decisions that will affect their futures. I dealt with this situation by holding a meeting with my direct subordinates as early as possible. I generally insisted that it happen on the first day of my tenure.

The purpose of the meeting was to discuss how we were going to work together. My opening statement was a well-researched description of my understanding of the group's broad goals and mission. That was followed by a brief outline of my background, with some emphasis on the skills I possessed that might help the group to meet its goals and mission. I would then describe my management style. Finally, I would close with some personal information about my background and my family and with a description of my ethical standards. At the conclusion of the meeting, I would circulate a schedule to everyone at the meeting and request that each employee sign up for a one-hour meeting with me during the next two or three days. I would tell them that the purposes of the meeting were to get to know them, to understand their roles in the group, and to become familiar with their opinions. Simply put, the meeting would consist of three topics: the individual's background information, the individual's career goals and ambitions, and the individual's assessment of the strengths and weakness of the department.

I would adhere rigidly to the schedule until all of the interviews were conducted. These interviews were most successful when I could engage the individuals to do most of the talking. People want to be helpful, and it certainly is sound management to understand the department from the perspective of the individuals who work there. It also gave me some understanding of each individual's attitudes and ambitions.

After accomplishing the interviews, I would hold a second group meeting to provide feedback. I would prioritize the issues that were raised in the first meeting and then open a discussion on each issue. We would agree on which individuals or groups would be responsible for resolving the issues. These issues would form the initial agenda of our weekly meetings. We were on our way.

I know other effective managers who have very different approaches. Many prefer to have one-on-one meetings with individual employees prior to holding the first group meeting. Others prefer to keep things running exactly the way they always have run and to take time to observe the department before implementing changes. The important point of this discussion is that you get only a single chance to start managing a group. Make a conscious decision about how you are going to assume control.

Replacing a particularly popular supervisor often presents problems. Many of your subordinates will suggest that your predecessor would have handled certain situations this way or that way, or your group may openly pine for the earlier supervisor. This is a natural human reaction. The former supervisor had the group in a comfort zone with minimum uncertainty. You represent the red zone of uncertainty. The only way to handle this situation is to work your way through it. Eventually, the group will become comfortable with your managerial style, and they will put the former supervisor at the back of their minds.

After assuming control of a group, it is your responsibility to keep it focused and on track. Faster than you can imagine, your life will become busy. The hierarchy above you will constantly challenge you to improve your group; this is referred to as the "what have you done for me lately?" syndrome. No one is going to let you rest on your laurels. Your peer group within the organization will try to off-load parts of their work in an attempt to improve their department's efficiency. Your subordinates will require your attention in order to maintain focus, efficiency, and interest. Good managers are time-efficient managers. Time efficiency is achieved by setting clear goals for each day and allocating sufficient time to each task. Reorder your goals every day. Here are some tips on time efficiency:

- No matter how tempting, do not do someone else's task. Often, it is just easier to do it yourself than to teach someone to do it. In the long run, however, it is far more efficient to teach someone to do a repetitive task than to do it yourself.

- Complete each task that you begin. A great amount of time is consumed when restarting a project.

- Answer phone calls and e-mails promptly. Get them out of the way.

- Run meetings efficiently. Most of what is accomplished in a meeting gets done in the first and last fifteen minutes. Thus, the ideal length of a meeting is thirty-one minutes. Have an agenda. Make people stick to an agenda. Cut off irrelevant points. Conclude an agenda with clear decisions about what is to be done, who will do it, and when it is to be completed. Minimize the number of people at meetings by including only those people who influence the subject.

- Be efficient in your conversations. Stick to the subject, and end conversations when topics have been thoroughly vetted.

- Keep a diary, and examine it at the end of the week. Look for areas where your time was used inefficiently, and avoid those situations in the future.

- Do not overcommit yourself to work. Your efficiency goes down if you do not have balance in your life.

Stay in touch with your subordinates. The most important part of managing people is to communicate with them. As a supervisor, you should always strive to minimize uncertainty for your subordinates. That does not mean that you should coddle them. They are adults and will accept bad news as well as good news; thus, a forthright and open approach is valuable. Do not delay in passing news along to subordinates; the informal information system in any organization is often much faster than the formal system. Your subordinates may already know what you are going to tell them, but they will be grateful if they are among the first to receive official notification.

The most challenging subordinates will be from the two extremes of the spectrum: the very ambitious and the highly unmotivated. The ambitious will want as much face time with you as possible and will be continually seeking to network and improve themselves. Assuming that you are doing the same things, it is often easy to agree with them to share information about opportunities. Such alliances can be helpful in forwarding one's own career. The unmotivated subordinates are more difficult. My approach was to try to improve the performance of each unmotivated individual through short-term goal setting. We would sit together and set goals on either a weekly or a monthly basis, depending on the severity of the situation. Then, we would meet weekly to review progress. During each goal-setting exercise, we would try to stretch the individual's workload. We would continue this until the employee improved or was not able to reach an adequate level of performance.

Dismissing people is a very hard thing to do. One of the best pieces of advice in my career came from a senior executive at McCann-Erickson, a large advertising agency. We were at lunch, and I was sharing with him a problem that I was having with an employee. General Motors had invested a good deal of money in training this employee, but he was not performing up to his potential. The executive suggested that I fire the employee. I was shocked and asked why he recommended such drastic action. He said, "If you know that this person is not going to be able to succeed at General Motors, you are wasting time that the employee could be spending building a career in another industry. Basically, you are stealing the employee's future by condemning him to continue pursuing a mediocre career in your industry. People need to find a fit in order to do their best." That advice has served me well over the course of my career. Every time I have had to dismiss an employee, it has been difficult to do. But I was able to sleep at night because I knew that I had worked with the employee one-on-one to try to improve performance and had determined that the person's talents were best applied to other pursuits. As a supervisor, you have a responsibility to the people who are pulling their weight in your group to weed out the people who are not pulling their weight.

Finally, do not get in over your level of competence with an employee. Some employees may have serious problems outside of work. In your career, you may have subordinates who are alcoholics, drug addicts, or battered spouses, or you may have employees who are mentally unstable. Unless you are trained to deal with these problems, get help from a professional. The first place to turn to is the human resources department if you suspect that a subordinate has serious personal problems. In some large institutions, there may be trained counselors who can deal directly with the problems. In most other cases, employers will have access to professionals who can help the employee. Attempting to take on such problems by yourself is irresponsible because you do not have the training and experience to counsel this person. Compassion and support, however, are always appropriate responses.

Budgetary Resources

The annual budget cycle is one of the most important concerns for managers in any institution. Earlier, I made the case that institutions rely on the ability of the management to focus the resources and successfully complete the mission. The budget is the most basic and important tool that management has for performing those tasks.

Historically, budget decisions were top-down events. Management predicted how much money would come into the institution for the next several years and then decided how much they could spend and still make a profit. Management allocated money to each department based on their sense of what was needed. Departments then operated, as best they could, within these budgets.

In most institutions today, budget decisions are bottom-up events. Sometime in the middle of the year, senior management requests that managers forecast revenues for the next several years. In a for-profit organization, this forecast focuses on the next year's sales. In a charitable organization, the forecast includes anticipated donations for the following year. In a governmental organization, budget decisions are based on the expected share of the next year's tax revenues. Senior management then agrees on the revenue forecast for the following year. That forecast could be more or less than the current year's budget.

After receiving the revenue forecasts, departments are asked to determine their cash-operating needs. At the for-profit businesses in which I have worked, the first round of forecasted operating needs usually exceeds the available revenue and thereby produces a projected loss. Obviously, it is unacceptable for an institution to approve a budget beyond its expected revenues, so a series of internal negotiations, called budget reviews, take place. Managers are asked to defend their budgets and to assist the management in paring the budget down to an acceptable size.

The role of supervisors in this process is fairly clear. It is their responsibility to prepare a clear picture of their operating needs. In this budget, they are most concerned with the items that are vital to the operation of their units. These items might include salary increases, headcount increases, expenses for materials, and any discretionary funds for activities such as travel and advertising. Items such as rent, heat, and light are allocated to the group based on some formula adopted by the finance department. These formulas are usually perceived as unfair but are seldom open to negotiation. The supervisor should spend a great deal of time preparing the rationale for each item, because he or she will be called upon to defend the budget in the budget review. As in any negotiation, preparation is the key, as is a clear feeling for where compromise can be reached. A supervisor that can deliver a solid budget, and then accept a reasonable compromise, will be viewed favorably by bosses and subordinates.

CHAPTER X

Negotiation

Like it or not, you are a negotiator. Negotiation is a fact of life.
Roger Fisher and William Ury, *Getting to Yes*, Penguin Books, 1991

The intents of this chapter are to give you some rough guidelines for conducting negotiations and to help you recognize some of the tactics that may be employed by unscrupulous negotiators. I would, however, recommend that each of you take the time to read two excellent books authored by members of the Harvard Negotiation Project:

- *Getting to Yes*, Roger Fisher and William Ury, Penguin Press, 1991, ISBN 0-140-15735-2

- *Getting past No*, William Ury, Bantam Books, 1993, ISBN 0-553-37131-2

Negotiation is a technique that we use every day, but we often feel uneasy about it. We have been using it since we were born. We got hungry and made a loud, screeching noise, and then someone fed us. We learned that we could gain things by making loud, screeching noises. As we grew older, our techniques became more sophisticated. Once we began to speak, we learned to plead: "Mommy, please buy this, and I promise to be a good boy or girl." Then we would beg: "Please, please, Mommy—I really want this, and I'll never ask for anything else." Then, we would fall back on the loud, screeching noise technique. We often got our way, but we rarely kept our part of the bargain by being a good boy or girl.

Things became more complicated, and, around seven years of age, we learned to reason and use outside examples: "Dad, why can't I stay up and watch television? Mary's parents let her." "Mom, why do I have to be home at ten o'clock, when everyone else can stay out until midnight? I look like such a dork." Fortunately, the people with whom we negotiated, our parents, loved us and rarely used their considerable power and negotiating skills—unless they thought our welfare was at stake.

Types of Negotiations

There are two kinds of negotiation: distributive and integrative. Distributive negotiation occurs when there is a fixed set of resources and the outcome is based on who gets the greatest amount of resources. Most people visualize negotiations in this way. The goal of a distributive negotiation is to get more than one's fair share. Distributive negotiation is often referred to as "win-lose" negotiation.

During integrative negotiation, the negotiators are not constrained by a concept of fixed resources to be divided. Rather, they take the approach that, by understanding each person's point of view, they may be able to achieve satisfactory outcomes for all parties. Integrative negotiation is often referred to as "win-win" negotiation.

Steps in Negotiation

Goal Setting

The first step in negotiations is to understand what you are trying to achieve. The clearest goals are ones that are measurable—for example, the number of dollars, size, weight, or quality. Measurable goals are often expressed as ranges with minimums and maximums. Goals may also be clear but not measurable—for example, a better quality of life, more security, or a better work environment. Once clear goals are established, it is important to look at alternative paths for achieve these goals. Fisher and Ury discuss the idea of a "BATNA" in their book. BATNA stands for "Best Alternative to a Negotiated Agreement." This is a negotiator's walk-away position, a point where a negotiator will terminate a negotiation and choose an alternative path to his or her goals. A goal might be to purchase reliable cars that will last five years for $18,000.

Preparation

"Most negotiations are won or lost even before the talking begins, depending on the quality of preparation."[1] Information gives you the advantage in any negotiation. Most people are often too lazy or time constrained to prepare, and they end up getting shortchanged in a negotiation. Information on most subjects is readily available on the World Wide Web. In Appendix B, there is an example that illustrates how to gather information when purchasing an automobile.

Setting the Negotiating Environment

Success in negotiations can often be defined by who controls the environment. One of the best examples of this is an automobile negotiation. A car salesperson will attempt to control an unprepared buyer and lead the buyer to purchase a vehicle that yields the highest profit for the dealership. A prepared buyer can easily negate this advantage, as shown in Appendix B. Setting the environment means defining such details as the following:

- The venue where the negotiations will take place
- The agenda for the negotiations
- The time available to complete the negotiations
- The final decision makers in the negotiations
- The preparer of the final agreement

---

1. *Getting past No*, William Ury, Bantam Press, p. 16.

Negotiating

The type of negotiation will be defined early in the process. Persons desiring an integrative negotiation will be open and trusting. Progress will be slow in the beginning as both sides earn each other's trust and expose their needs. As positions become clear, brainstorming will occur, resulting in new solutions and ideas. Eventually a consensus will emerge.

Persons entering a distributive negotiation will be guarded and protective of their information. They will use information to refute their opponent's position and attempt to gain a bigger piece of the pie for themselves. These negotiations will be a series of give-and-take, often with high emotional content in the discussions.

Closing the Deal

Once agreement is reached, it is very important to define all the agreed conditions. In a high-stakes negotiation, these conditions need to be put in writing. Often lawyers will finalize these types of agreements in binding contracts. In less formal negotiations, it is important to close the deal in a timely fashion. This ensures that neither party will begin to have second thoughts and makes it less likely that the negotiations will need to be reopened.

Unsavory Tactics

Negotiation has been around since humans learned to speak. Societies and cultures have many different norms and standards for negotiations. Like most human processes, some unsavory tactics have evolved. I am presenting these tactics because, as a negotiator, you need to be able to fend them off. I consider these tactics to be unscrupulous and urge you not to use them.

- The intimidation tactic. This is where a negotiator projects an aggressive and unreasonable personality, in hopes of achieving appeasement. Often in this scenario the hostile negotiator will engage in personal attacks. The solution to this type of tactic is to insist on some behavioral norms or walk away from the negotiation.

- Lowball or highball. The negotiator will offer a highly deflated or inflated offer. It is known in several trades as bottom-fishing or highballing. Of all the hardball tactics, this is the one that has shown to be effective in creating value from the offer. The best way to counter this tactic is by focusing your preparation on clearly understanding the financial value of the transaction.

- Cheating and lying. These tactics involve creating facts that don't exist, misrepresenting facts, bargaining with no intention of reaching a solution, or overwhelming the other party with a multitude of facts. Negotiation preparations can usually pierce through these tactics.

- Unreasonable time constraints. This technique involves putting stress on the other negotiators to decide before a certain deadline. This tactic is often used in labor negotiations, with strike deadlines. A variation of this technique, developed in the last century in international commerce, involved asking a negotiator when his or her plane was departing. The local party would then defer discussing key issues until a few hours before the scheduled departure, in an effort to gain concessions because of the person's desire to catch his or her plane. The way to counter this tactic is not to disclose any personal time constraints.

- Good cop–bad cop. This technique is used in interrogating prisoners. One negotiator is openly hostile to the suspect, while a second tries to seem reasonable and rational. The bad cop will eventually leave the negotiations for some made-up purpose; going to the bathroom is a frequently used excuse. The good cop will then make a special offer, urging the negotiating party to accept it in order to avoid further confrontation with the hostile negotiator. When you spot a good cop–bad cop negotiation, simply call your adversaries' bluff, tell them that you know what is going on, and explain that you will not continue to negotiate until the bad cop is removed or becomes reasonable. Continuing to negotiate in a good cop–bad cop environment will embolden the bad cop to present greater and more unreasonable demands.

- The Trojan horse or bogey. In this tactic, a negotiator makes a demand that he or she does not value at all, in hopes of conceding that demand for something significant that the negotiator does want. Basically, the negotiator gives away something that has no value to him or her or that he or she never expected to receive for something that has value to the negotiator. When you spot this tactic, again, explain calmly that you know what is going on, and leave the negotiations if the opposition does not change its behavior.

- Nibble. This tactic involves requesting further small concessions after the parties have agreed to terms. This is a tactic often employed in real estate transactions. Buyers often request allowances for perceived or small deficiencies in the real estate just before the closing. Depending on the magnitude of the request and the situation of the real estate market, sellers may often grant small concessions.

- Take it or leave it. This tactic is often used by high-pressure salespeople. It is what is called a closing tactic. Salespeople make money by the number of sales they are responsible for; thus, time is money. Countering this tactic requires a good BATNA and the time to seek the other alternatives. It is probable that you will still be able to get the same deal at a later time.

- Exploding offer. In this technique, the negotiator explains that the offer is good for only a limited time. The negotiator argues that the negotiations will start from the beginning after the offer explodes. To counter this tactic, say that it is of no concern to you, you are checking other alternatives (your BATNA), and you will get back to the negotiator when you are ready.

- Split the difference. This is a tactic that seems particularly effective in the United States. It can be a method of resolving negotiations quickly but often at a significant price if one of the participants has employed the highball/lowball tactic. The way to deal with it is to understand value, and simply state that splitting the difference is too easy a way to arrive at an agreement in a negotiation as important as this one.

In summary, a good negotiator has several important traits. The negotiator must have faith in his or her abilities and in his or her preparation. The negotiator must believe in the opponent's willingness to reach a solution and be open-minded in seeking creative solutions. Finally, a good negotiator understands the alternatives to reaching a solution and is willing to walk away from the negotiations when they are deadlocked. If you wish to learn more about becoming a good negotiator, please spend some time reading the two books listed at the beginning of this chapter. Negotiating is a very important skill for building a successful career.

CHAPTER XI

Random Thoughts

> This above all: to thine own self be true,
> And it must follow, as the night the day,
> Thou canst not then be false to any man.
> William Shakespeare (1564–1616), British poet, *Hamlet* (I. iii)

> Have you been able to think out and manage your own life? You
> have done the greatest task of all ... All other things, ruling,
> hoarding, building, are only little appendages and props, at most.
> Michel de Montaigne (1533–92), French essayist, "Of Experience,"
> *The Essays (Les Essais)*, bk. III, ch. 13, Abel Langelier, Paris (1595)

There are a number of subjects that I consider very important but
that did not seem to fit elsewhere.

Be True to Yourself

One of the hardest lessons in my life has been to learn that when
undesirable things happen, it is not someone else's fault. In my
early adult years, it was convenient and easy to rationalize failure or
misfortune as not my fault. Eventually, with a great deal of help
from my wife, I began to understand that if I truly believed that I
could control events, then I was, therefore, accountable for the outcomes. Your quality of life improves when you can understand your

faults and admit your failures but continue to move forward and make decisions. Try to be as honest with yourself as you possibly can, and learn to trust loved ones when they point out flaws. The flaws that you most aggressively deny are the ones that are the greatest stumbling blocks to your happiness.

Practice Ethical Behavior

Ethical behavior is the most desirable trait that I seek in a friend or colleague. Persons who have a strong sense of right and wrong and strive for ethical behavior have a great advantage in life. First, they do not have to attempt to maintain a web of deceit, which is a very difficult thing to do. Second, they sleep better at night, because they are secure in their belief that they have dealt fairly in their relationships.

Maintain Your Physical Health

As an adult, you now have exclusive custody of your body. It deserves regular attention. There are several simple steps that you can follow to maintain and enhance your physical health.

- Exercise regularly. This means, at a minimum, an hour of vigorous exercise three times a week. During part of my career, I was traveling internationally about 90 percent of the time and living in hotels fifteen to twenty days a month. Not all hotels were equipped with gyms, so I would get up an hour early, usually at 5:30 AM, and power walk around the city. It is interesting to see such cities as Brussels, Madrid, Tokyo, and Beijing in the early morning. You will benefit mentally and physically from regular exercise. All it takes is a little self-discipline.

- Watch your diet. When I graduated from college, I weighed 180 pounds and ate everything in sight. Today, I weigh around 200 pounds and try to watch what I eat. As your body's metabolism slows down in your late twenties or early thirties, you burn fewer calories, and you need less to eat.

Obesity is becoming a major problem in the United States. Keys to a good diet are the following:

o Plenty of fresh fruit and vegetables

o Eating smaller portions more frequently throughout the day, starting with a healthy breakfast

o Dramatic reductions in fast foods and sugar

o Regular exercise

- Watch your alcohol consumption. It may have been fun to experiment with alcohol during your college years. Many of us, me included, often have consumed too much alcohol during our college years. Unfortunately, alcohol is addictive and can have serious consequences if consumed in excess. Slow down—drink to relax, not to get drunk. Moderate your alcohol use.

- Stop smoking. Since I returned to campus life, the number of young people who smoke has shocked me. Although alcohol may be consumed in moderation for the rest of your life, smoking causes cancer. No rational person who is a conscientious custodian of his or her body would smoke. Stop now.

Minimize the Stress in Your Life

As a college student, you are all too familiar with stress. I once read that the most frequent dream had by college graduates is the nightmare of missing an exam or of forgetting to turn in a paper. The article said that these dreams prevail for as long as ten years after graduation. This is certainly an indication of the stress induced by the rigors of a college education.

Life after college becomes even more stressful. As this book has shown, there are a myriad of issues to deal with simultaneously. There are several keys for me in dealing with stress:

- Work on understanding uncertainty and moderating its effects. Uncertainty causes stress; facing issues and sharing them with others can reduce stress.

- Give yourself quiet time. Regularly get away. Take a walk, or sit in a quiet room. Go to a church, temple, or mosque and think. Reorder your life, and deal with the most stressful items first.

- Don't second-guess your decisions. Among the greatest causes of stress in the world are the "would have," "could have," and "should have" regrets.

- Get regular exercise. It has the physical effect of releasing tension from muscles.

- Get enough sleep.

- Stay away from stimulants, such as coffee and drugs, which speed up the metabolism.

- Share your problems. Tell partners, friends, and parents about your problems. The act of sharing problems with people relieves some of the burden that we perceive we are carrying.

- Recreate. Have some fun. All work and no play makes for a dull person. After all, you are working hard in order to enjoy your life.

Relationships

The greatest joys in my journey are the people who journey with me. My wife and I have journeyed together for over thirty-five years, and our two sons have joined us for nearly thirty years. Countless friends, business associates, and students have accompanied me for shorter periods. Each person, in his or her own way, has enriched my journey and enhanced the quality of my life. Two of the great challenges of life are finding the right people to journey with and succeeding in getting them to add you to their journeys.

A few things that I have learned about relationships are the following:

- In close, intimate relationships (such as those with a spouse, child, or good friend), it is all about giving. The more you give to a relationship, the more interesting and happy your journey. As soon as you begin to think about taking instead of giving, the relationship is doomed.

- I enter all relationships by assuming that my partners are trustworthy and honest. When these assumptions are betrayed, I quickly lose interest in the relationship.

- In intimate relationships, don't be afraid to express your own feelings and points of view. Mature discussions about differences, when conducted with respect for your partner, often get issues that are degrading the relationship out into the open. Also, it is wonderful to make up after an argument.

Finally, thanks to anyone who has made it this far through the book. The book should be an evolving thing, and it is my hope to make it better and to keep it current. If you have any suggestions or comments, please contact me at pwallace@stonehill.edu.

APPENDIX A

Credit Card Example

Let's say that you have run up $1,000 worth of credit card debt. Let's also suppose that you are content to make the minimum monthly payment, but you want to understand what that means.

Go to http://www.bankrate.com, and follow these steps:

1. Click on CREDIT CARDS.

2. In the box titled CALCULATOR, click on PAYING THE MINIMUM.

3. Type your credit card balance in the appropriate box. We will use $1,000.

4. Type your interest rate in the appropriate box (you can find it on your credit card bill). We will use 14 percent.

5. Enter your current minimum payment. We will use $25.

6. Press the CALCULATE button. The answer I got was that it will take 123 months—10 years and 3 months—to pay off the credit card and that we would have paid $666.96 in interest for the $1,000.00 that we borrowed.

Car Loan Example

Let's walk through another example. Again, if you have Internet access, it might be valuable to walk through this example.

Go to http://www.bankrate.com, and follow these steps:

1. Click on AUTOS.

2. In the section titled CALCULATORS, click on VIEW MORE CALCU-LATORS.

3. Click on HOW MUCH CAR CAN YOU AFFORD?

4. Enter your name.

5. Enter your after-tax monthly income. We will use the $2,156 we used in Chapter IV.

6. If you are currently making car payments, follow the other menu. For this example, I have assumed that we are currently making no payments.

7. The financial model suggests that we spend $323 on car payments. It is lower than the $377 that we had in the budget. Maybe we can free up some cash in the budget here.

8. I said that we would put down $1,000, that we would finance it for five years (sixty months), and that we would pay the current rate prevailing in March 2007 (6.97 percent). The Web site told me that we could buy a car worth $17,344. That's only $2,000 less than we were going to pay for the car in the budget, and we save more than $50 a month.

Mortgage Example

Go to http://www.bankrate.com, and follow these steps:

1. Click on MORTGAGES.

2. On the left-hand side, you will be able to enter your data.

3. Enter $135,000 in the loan amount box. This is the $150,000 that we will pay for our dwelling, minus our $15,000 down payment.

4. Because the bank will lend us the money for thirty years and because we want the lowest payments possible, enter a thirty-year term.

5. Use the average rate prevailing at the time. We'll use 5.68 percent, which was the prevailing rate quoted in March 2007.

6. The payment I obtained was $781.83. This is a little less than the amount that we are paying for our half of the rent in the urban budget scenario.

APPENDIX B

Automobile Purchase Negotiation

You want to purchase a car. The first consideration in goal setting is to define how much you can spend. In Chapter V on financial leverage, we used http://www.bankrate.com and decided that we could spend around $18,000 for a new car. Because you are going to pay taxes and licensing fees, this probably means that you should be looking for a negotiated price of around $17,000. A second goal you might consider is that we want a reliable car, one that will last five years.

With these goals in mind, you enter the preparation phase. Because this is the second-most-expensive purchase (the most expensive will be your owner-occupied dwelling), you need to put some time and effort into research.

Are you going to buy a new car or a used car? How are you going to establish reliability? How are you going to deal with the price issue? You can answer these questions and many more at one of the excellent Web sites that contain pricing information. The choices include *Kelley Blue Book* at http://www.kbb.com, *Edmunds* at http://www.edmunds.com, and *NADA Guides* at http://www.nadaguides.com. At the *Kelley Blue Book* Web site in July 2005, I found several new cars in your price range: the Kia Spectra 5 at around $16,000, the Saturn Ion 3 at around $15,700, the Honda Accord DX at around $17,600, and the Toyota Corolla LE at around $16,330. After checking the quality ratings on the same Web site, you might decide to eliminate the Kia and Saturn because of relatively low ratings. The Honda Accord DX and the Toyota Corolla remained as possible choices.

Buying a used car is a bit more challenging than buying a new car because of the risk involved. However, because of the popularity of leasing, it is possible to get vehicles with about 30,000 to 35,000 miles, which should give five years of reliable service. While scrolling through *Kelley's* used car values, I found the following: a 2000 Acura TL for $15,620, a 2004 Chrysler Concord for $15,065, a 2003 Mazda 6 for $15,485, and a 2000 BMW 3 series for $17,250. So, the research has yielded a sufficient number of choices.

To review used car quality and reliability, I turned to *Consumer Reports* at http://www.consumerreports.org. There is a small annual fee to join this Web site, but it is worth it. Every major item that you will buy—stereo, TV, mattress, car—has been tested and rated by it. *Consumer Reports* is free of any commercial sponsorship and, thus, is unbiased. Using this Web site to prepare for purchases should save you a good deal of money and hassle. All four of the used cars had good reliability records, so my list of cars would include them. Thus, you have six candidate cars to research more closely.

You now want to establish the key prices for the cars. You want the dealer price for the new cars and the trade-in value for the used cars. The trade-in value is approximately what the dealer paid for the used car, and the retail value is the price for which the dealer expects to sell the used car. The difference between the two is the dealer's profit opportunity. All the necessary data is available on the *Kelley Blue Book* Web site.

You can put together a spreadsheet, which might look like the table shown below.

Car Make	Dlr. Price	List Price	Trade-in Value	Sale Price	Dlr. Profit
NEW					
Honda DX	$15,907	$17,610		$16,201	$294
Toyota LE	$14,837	$16,330		$15,198	$361
USED					
'00 Accura TL			$11,455	$15,620	$4,165
'04 Chrysler	$8,290		$9,220	$15,065	$5,845
'03 Mazda 6	$11,085		$10,765	$15,485	$4,720
'00 BMW 3			$13,340	$17,250	$3,910

A quick examination of the chart shows that you have much more latitude for negotiation with a used car than with a new car. The greater spread in used car prices is a function of the many variables that affect the value of used cars. The major factors in used car value are the age of the car, the mileage on the car, the condition of the car, and whether the car has been in an accident. Much of this information is available for a specific car at http://www.carfax.com, the Web site of Car Fax.

Let's consider a scenario in which you are trying to buy a car. This is a typical distributive negotiation, but let us see how we can turn it into an integrative negotiation.

You are prepared to discuss your purchase with a dealer salesperson. You should have already contacted your bank, arranged for a loan, and acquired a clear understanding of the interest rate and monthly payments. The first step in establishing your bargaining position is to make it clear to the salesperson that you are well informed. You do this by stating that you intend to buy a new Honda Accord DX and that it is the only car that interests you. The salesperson almost always tries to show the luxury model, instead of the base model, of the car. Car buyers need to be firm and stick to their guns. Remember that you are trying to use your information to establish your bargaining position. The salesperson will typically ask for your address and phone number, and, when you take a test drive, he or she will make a copy of your driver's license. These are all acceptable requests, but you should expect to get follow-up phone calls. You should test-drive the car. If you are interested, you should make a low but reasonable offer. For example, in the case of the Honda, you know that the dealer price is $15,407 and that these cars are currently selling in your area for $15,638. You might say, "I know that the dealer price is around $15,400, and I am willing to offer you $15,500."

The salesperson is likely to try several hostile negotiating tactics at this point. "Who told you the dealer price? You're way off base; you don't know what you're talking about." These histrionics are almost a necessity for car salespeople. Their pay, generally, is tied to the quantity of cars they sell and to the profit they deliver on each car sold. Car buyers must stick to their guns and weather the storm, but if the salesperson will not get serious, they should move on to another Honda dealer.

One favorite salesperson tactic is to pretend that he needs to talk to the boss. After a brief pause, the boss and the salesperson reappear, and the boss lays a guilt trip on the car buyer: "What are you trying to do to this nice salesperson? Are you trying to get him fired? Why did you come in here with all this wrong information from the Internet?" Secure negotiators will restate their offers, and, faced with this situation, the boss will oftentimes begin serious negotiation. In our scenario, the boss might say, "The best deal I can offer you is $15,800." You now have a floor of $15,500 and a ceiling of $15,800, and it is time to leave. You should shop the other dealers and car choices and then go home and spend some time deciding what you really want to do. Make your final selection, and return to the dealer of your choice; you will conduct the final negotiations by working between the previously established floors and ceilings. When you return to the dealership, the salesperson will realize that you are a serious buyer and that he can achieve his goal of selling a car. At the point where both parties see that they can achieve their goals, you have succeeded in turning the negotiation into an integrative negotiation.

During the final negotiations, the salesperson will try to expand his profit opportunities by trying to sell you all kinds of extras: floor mats, undercoating, extended warranties, roof racks, and so on. A car buyer rarely needs any of this equipment and, in most cases, can buy it elsewhere for less money. Finally, the dealer can often make money by offering financing and insurance. The dealer may have a subsidized financing offer that is worth considering, but, generally, bank financing is more attractive than dealer financing. Insurance is better secured through a reputable agent.

In summation, the preparation that went into your negotiations for a car led to an integrative negotiation with the salesperson and dealer because you were so well informed. You can be equally successful with a dealer if you have a trade-in, but this situation involves a good deal more arithmetic. This is another reason to visit several dealers, work the numbers when you get home, and find the true cost of the deal. In a recent car purchase, I achieved about a $6,000 price differential by shopping at several car dealerships. The preparation for these negotiations took about twenty hours, and the negotiations took about ten hours. It worked out to a reward of about $200 an hour ($6,000 divided by thirty hours).

ABOUT THE AUTHOR

Peter Wallace has an impressive record as a business executive and teacher. Wallace started his career with General Motors and rose through the international marketing ranks to head General Motors' operations for U.S. car sales in Europe. During his career, Wallace acquired companies in the United States for the Swiss company Electrowatt AG; he became chairman and chief executive officer of two of these companies. He retired in 1997 from ITT Corporation, where he was a senior vice president of the World Directories unit. Wallace was noted for his ability to mentor and develop young talent for executive positions.

In 1999, Stonehill College—ranked by *U.S. News and World Report* as number one in its Best Northern Comprehensive Colleges—Bachelor's category—invited Peter Wallace to teach its capstone business course. As an associate professor of business administration, Wallace received the Outstanding Faculty Member Award in 2003. He has worked with over one thousand college seniors and helped them prepare for the transition to professional careers. He has synthesized the experience that he gained in climbing the corporate ladder into a series of lectures on how to cope with life after college. One student dubbed the lectures "the www (Wallace's Words of Wisdom) lectures." As the result of many students' requests, he has organized these lectures into a book. Wallace also teaches courses in international business and in decision making and negotiation.

Peter Wallace holds a bachelor of science degree in industrial management from the University of Rochester and a master of business administration degree from Inter American University, and he completed the Senior International Management program at Harvard Business School. He and his wife, Annabelle, have traveled extensively and have lived in Switzerland, Belgium, and Brazil. Wallace speaks five languages and served as an officer in the United States Coast Guard from 1965 to 1969.

978-1-58348-107-3
1-58348-107-9

34449369R00075

Made in the USA
San Bernardino, CA
28 May 2016